CYBERWARFARE: TERROR AT A CLICK

DATE DUE

DEMCO INC 38-2971

CYBERWARFARE: TERROR AT A CLICK

JOHN V. BLANE (ED.)

Novinka Books
New York

Senior Editors: Susan Boriotti and Donna Dennis
Coordinating Editor: Tatiana Shohov
Office Manager: Annette Hellinger
Graphics: Wanda Serrano
Book Production: Matthew Kozlowski, Jonathan Rose and Jennifer Vogt
Circulation: Cathy DeGregory, Ave Maria Gonzalez and Raheem Miller
Communications and Acquisitions: Serge P. Shohov

Library of Congress Cataloging-in-Publication Data
Available Upon Request

ISBN 1-56072-996-1

Copyright © 2002 by Novinka Books
    An Imprint of Nova Science Publishers, Inc.
    227 Main Street, Suite 100
    Huntington, New York 11743
    Tele. 631-424-(NOVA) 6682   Fax 631-425-5933
    E Mail Novascil@aol.com

CONTENTS

CYBERWARFARE

Steven A. Hildreth

INTRODUCTION

Background

There is a war being waged in cyberspace[1] today – at least that's what many in government and the media would have us believe. Former Deputy Secretary of Defense John Hamre testified to Congress, for example, "you can basically say we are at war."

A couple of years ago, the Central Intelligence Agency (CIA) only mentioned Russia and China specifically as possible cyber threats. Today, U.S. officials indicate that more than 20 countries have various kinds of information operations (IO) directed against the United States. The CIA

---

[1] *Cyberspace* is the total interconnectedness of human beings through computers and telecommunication without regard to physical geography. William Gibson is sometimes credited with inventing or popularizing the term by using it in his novel of 1984, *Neuromancer*. [http://www.whatis.com/WhatIs_Definition_Page/0,4152,211883,00.html] Cyberspace is often used as a metaphor for describing the non-physical terrain created by computer systems. Online systems, for example, create a cyberspace within which people can communicate with one another (via e-mail), do research, or simply window shop. Like physical space, cyberspace contains objects (files, mail messages, graphics, etc.) and different modes of transportation and delivery. Unlike real space, though, exploring cyberspace does not require any physical movement other than pressing keys on a keyboard or moving a mouse. Some programs, particularly computer games, are designed to create a special cyberspace, one that resembles physical reality in some ways but defies it in others. In its extreme form, called virtual reality, users are presented with visual, auditory, and even tactile feedback that makes cyberspace feel real. See, for example, [http://aol.pcwebopedia.com/TERM/c/cyberspace.html].

testified more recently that adversaries are incorporating cyberwarfare[2] as a new part of their military doctrine. A declassified Navy threat assessment identifies Russia, China, India, and Cuba as countries who have acknowledged policies of preparing for cyberwarfare and who are rapidly developing their capabilities. North Korea, Libya, Iran, Iraq, and Syria reportedly have some capability, and France, Japan, and Germany are active in this field.[3]

The media and others often also warn of cyberterrorists waiting for the right moment to bring down the U.S. power, transportation, or communications grids. For example, at a hearing of the Joint Economic Committee on cyberterrorism that included the CIA (Feb. 23, 2000), Sen. Bob Bennett said, "attacks on American defense and industrial facilities in cyberspace are as real and dangerous as any conventional threat to economic prosperity and national security."

But is all this really war or warfare? Computer systems at the Pentagon and other military sites get "attacked" thousands of times each year. But is it war if many or most of those attacks come from teenagers here in the United States, or even abroad? Does the military even *know* how many of those attacks it should genuinely be worried about? Is an attempt by a foreign nation to collect military secrets via the Internet or modem an act of war for which the United States is prepared to respond coercively? Should the United States respond in kind by waging war in cyberspace? What constitutes victory in cyberspace? Or is spying traditionally considered something else, something less than war? If another nation systematically attacks U.S. business networks to steal trade secrets in support of its own economic interests or to pass those secrets on to their own corporation for competitive advantage, is that warfare? Does the answer change if the attacking nation is a U.S. ally or friend?

---

[2] A number of terms are used to describe the various aspects of defending and attacking information and computer networks, as well as denying an adversary's ability to do the same, or even dominating the information environment on the battlefield. These terms are more accurately defined later in the section on Terms & Definitions. Meanwhile, cyberwarfare in this report will be used broadly to refer to these various activities. More specifically, it can include computer or network penetration, denial-of-service attacks on computers and networks, equipment sabotage through cyberspace, sensor jamming, and even manipulating trusted information sources to condition or control an adversary's thinking.

[3] Navy Names Nations Posing Cyber Threats. *Defense Week.* September 5, 2000, p. 1. The Office of Naval Intelligence prepared the report.

So what is the appeal of cyberwarfare or information warfare? Why choose cyberwarfare over other forms of warfare of conflict? Many see that it provides a range of relatively anonymous, non-lethal options that can be applied at the speed of light and with relatively low risk of escalation or more direct forms of conflict. In one sense, it's a way for others to wage an asymmetrical conflict against the United States. The likelihood of getting caught, let alone incurring U.S. military might, may seem low compared to the possible benefits. The appeal of cyberwarfare to the United States could grow out of the larger U.S. trend over the past twenty years to minimize conflict casualties and maximize technological advantages while pursuing increasingly activist foreign and defense policy agendas.

Purpose

This report is designed to examine broad cyberwarfare issues and raise underlying questions. The report first summarizes some cases that illustrate real-world concerns many have with respect to cyberwarfare. It then discusses the current U.S. policy and organizational approaches to cyberwarfare. The report also examines foreign perspectives, the issue of cyberterrorism, and some reported instances of cyberwarfare. An appendix on terms and definitions is included at the end of the report. This report's focus is on cyberwarfare activities sponsored by nation-states, but includes cyberterrorism that is aimed at achieving political objectives at the national level.

It is important to point out that a large number of other kinds of cyber attacks take place regularly, but they will not be addressed by this report. In fact, these types of attacks are likely more frequent than state-sponsored activities or cyberterrorism. These other attacks or intrusions also are unauthorized attempts to access computers, computer controlled systems, or networks. These activities can range from simply penetrating a system and examining it for the challenge, thrill, or interest, to entering a system for revenge, to steal information, cause embarrassment, extort money, or cause deliberate localized harm to computers or damage to a much larger infrastructure, such as a water supply or energy system. These cyber attacks might be referred to as hacking, cyber mischief, cyber hooliganism, person or corporate theft, revenge, or espionage, or organized crime activities (foreign and domestic). The realm for their resolution may lie in law enforcement and judicial systems, and legislative remedy where necessary.

Obviously, Congress plays a key role in the formulation, funding, conduct, and oversight of U.S. national security. The interplay of Congress and the Executive Branch on cyberwarfare issues in recent years is touched on later.

NATURE OF THE CHALLENGE: CASE STUDIES

Several examples help illustrate the complexity of cyberwarfare, as well as the concern that many have. They show the difficulty in identifying the source and purpose of the attack, in determining whether a coordinated attack is underway, in assessing what seems to work and what does not, and calculating the damages incurred. The cases summarized below help raise an important question: does cyberwar represent a fundamentally new form of 21st century warfare, for which the United States may or may not be prepared, or is it simply a new tool for traditional asymmetric conflict, for which this country also may or may not be prepared to manage?

Air Force Rome Lab (1994)

In March 1994, system administrators at Rome Lab in New York found their network under attack. The Air Force dispatched two teams to investigate further. The attacks were traced to an ISP (Internet Service Provider) first in New York, then in Seattle, Washington, where the Internet path dead-ended (the attackers used dial-up lines). There was subsequent monitoring at Rome Lab and two hacker handles or aliases were identified – Kuji and Datastream Cowboy. Informants were solicited and someone recognized a hacker from the United Kingdom; this hacker had bragged that he had broken into various U.S. military systems. The United States then contacted Scotland Yard. Scotland Yard discovered the hacker was "phreaking"[4] through Columbia and Chile to New York, defrauding telephone companies and the New York ISP as a jumping off point to attack Rome Lab. The UK hacker was later observed targeting other sites such as NATO headquarters, Goddard Space Flight Center, and Wright-Patterson Air Force Base. At least eight countries were used as conduits for these attacks. Scotland Yard had enough information to issue an arrest warrant

---

[4] Closely related to hacking, it means using a computer or other device to trick a phone system. Typically, phreaking is used to make free calls or to have calls charged to a different account.

and proceeded to make the arrest after data from the South Korean Atomic Research Institution was accessed. In all, over 150 intrusions were monitored at Rome Lab from 100 different points of origin. More than 100 other victims reportedly were hit. Datastream Cowboy, a 16 year-old British student, pled guilty and was fined. His mentor, Kuji, a 22 year-old Israeli technician, was found not guilty because no laws in Israel applied to this incident.

Eligible Receiver (1997)

Eligible Receiver was the first Information Warfare (IW) exercise in this country. Thirty-five people participated on the Red Team over 90 days using off-the-shelf technology and software. The scenario was a rogue state rejecting direct military confrontation with the United States, while seeking to attack vulnerable U.S. information systems. Some of the goals of the rogue state were to conceal the identity of the attackers and to delay or deny any U.S. ability to respond militarily. A number of cyber attacks (all simulated) were made against power and communications networks in Oahu, Los Angeles, Colorado Springs, and St. Louis, Chicago, Detroit, Washington, DC, Fayetteville, and Tampa.

Although reliable, unclassified results are hard to come by it is generally believed government and commercial sites were easily attacked and taken down. This exercise served as a wake-up call for many. Gen. Campbell, head of the Pentagon's Joint Task Force – Computer Network defense, wrote Eligible Receiver "clearly demonstrated our lack of preparation for a coordinated cyber and physical attack on our critical military and civilian infrastructure."[5] Then Pentagon spokesman Kenneth Bacon said, "Eligible Receiver was an important and revealing exercise that taught us that we must be better organized to deal with potential attacks against our computer systems and information infrastructure." Sen. John Kyl said in 1998:

> Well, [cyberterrorism is] surprisingly easy. It's hard to quantify that in words, but there have been some exercises run recently. One that's been in the media, called Eligible

---

[5] IAnewsletter. Vol. 3, No. 4, p. 10.

Receiver, demonstrated in real terms how vulnerable the transportation grid, the electricity grid, and others are to an attack by, literally, hackers – people using conventional equipment, no "spook" stuff in other words.[6]

Solar Sunrise (1998)

In February 1998, a number of Department of Defense networks were attacked using a well-known vulnerability in the Solaris (UNIX-based) computer system. The attackers: probed Defense Department servers to see if the vulnerability existed; exploited the vulnerability and entered the system; planted a program to gather data; and then returned later to collect that data.

Some of the initial probe activities appeared to originate from Harvard University and the United Arab Emirates (UAE), moving on to Pearl Harbor and a number of Air Force bases: Kirtland, Lackland, Andrews, Columbus, Gunter, and Tyndall. Later intrusion activities were monitored from the UAE, Utah State University, and a commercial Internet web site to some of the same Air Force bases. Further activity was monitored at dozens of other U.S. military sites and universities. International activity was monitored in Germany, France, Israel, UAE, and Taiwan. Over 500 computer systems were compromised, including military, commercial, and educational sites, by attackers using only moderately sophisticated tools.

In the end, two California High School students were arrested and pled guilty. Their mentor, an 18 year-old Israeli, was also arrested and indicted.

Although the Department of Defense called it "the most organized and systematic attack to date," many dismissed its seriousness because "the Justice Department claimed that no classified information was compromised."[7] And details or precisely what the hackers did are not publicly available.

Lessons some have drawn, however, are that Solar Sunrise confirmed the findings of Eligible Receiver: U.S. information systems are vulnerable. Additionally, others indicate that various legal issues remain unresolved (e.g., statutory restrictions and competing investigative needs and privacy concerns that hinder searches), there are no effective indications and

---

[6] Interview on Cyberterrorism, U.S. Information Agency, November 1998.
[7] See [http://www.sans.org/newlook/resource/IDFAQ/solar_sunrise.html].

warnings system in place; intrusion detection systems are insufficient, and there is too much government bureaucracy that hinders an effective and timely response.

U.S. VIEWS AND EFFORTS

How adequately is the United States prepared to deal with these kinds of cyber threats, as well as more serious threats to national security through cyberspace? This section summarizes how the United States now approaches these issues. Although it appears the government is now thinking about cyberwarfare issues more than in the past, and appears better organized, it is not clear whether a national consensus has formed as will form as to whether cyber threats constitute serious national security threats requiring a clear national security response.

Despite formal pronouncements (see below), it appears the government holds two major views on this subject. One view suggests that cyber threats are primarily a national security problem in that major U.S. national interests and critical infrastructure are threatened. Historically, U.S. national military and diplomatic power has often been brought to bear to protect those interests. A case can also be made that cyber threats to the United States similarly threaten U.S. national interests. Another view holds that cyber threats should be handled primarily by civil or domestic authorities. A major concern here is over a strong military role within the borders of the United States (as opposed to outside the borders). In addition, a variety of privacy and civil liberties concerns also raise concern over a stronger military role. In the past, threats to the United States from abroad could mostly be countered abroad. But today we live in an age where geographic borders are easier to broach and do not even exist in cyberspace. This represents a new challenge to decision makers.

Executive Branch

Policy and Doctrine. Several forms of guidance help shape U.S. policy toward cyber attacks and cyberwarfare. The most recent White House report on National Security Strategy notes "we face threats to critical national infrastructures, which increasingly could take the form of a cyber attack in addition to physical attack or sabotage, and could originate from terrorist or criminal groups, as well as hostile states."[8] These annual reports play a major guiding role within the Executive Branch national security bureaucracy.

The Department of Defense plays a key role in defending U.S. interests in cyberspace. Various Defense Department directives provide guidance and define terms such as Information Operations and Information Assurance (see section on Terms & Definitions). For instance, the Joint Doctrine for Information Operations (Joint Pub 3-13, October 9, 1998) represents a key document in defining how U.S. joint forces use cyberwarfare to support U.S. military strategy. But much of what the military does in cyberspace today is an outgrowth of traditional views and approaches toward ensuring information security of InfoSec.

The military has been further guided by Joint Vision 2010 (JV-2010), a broad long-term strategic concept for joint military strategy and planning purposed promulgated by the Joint Chiefs of Staff. JV-2010 embraced information superiority and technological advantages designed to transform traditional war fighting. Its successor, JV-2020 (released May 30, 2000), extends the conceptual template established by JV-2010 to guide the continuing transformation of U.S. military forces. Among other thing, JV-2020 states:

> Changes in the information environment make information superiority a key enabler of the transformation of the operational capabilities of the joint force and the evolution of joint command and control.

Also, the Quadrennial Defense Review (QDR) stated that asymmetric forms of warfare, such as information warfare, will become increasingly prevalent in the world, adding:

> because of the prevalence of such capabilities in the hands of potential future adversaries and the likelihood that such adversaries would resort to such means in the face of overwhelming U.S. conventional dominance, U.S. forces must plan and prepare to fight and win major theater wars under such conditions.[9]

---

[8] The White House. A National Security Strategy for a New Century. December 1999.

[9] Department of Defense. *Report of the Quadrennial Defense Review.* May 1997.

In addition, Presidential Decision Directive No. 63 (PDD-63) established in May 1998 a national goal to protect the nation's critical infrastructure[10] by the year 2003. PDD-63 further states that any disruptions to infrastructures "be brief, infrequent, manageable, geographically isolated, and minimally detrimental to the welfare of the United States."[11] More recently, the White House National Plan for Information Systems Protections (Jan. 2000) seeks to further identify U.S. critical infrastructure vulnerabilities as part of a longer-term effort to find solutions through government and private sector cooperation.[12]

Organization. Among a number of things, PDD-63 established the position of National Coordinator for Security, Infrastructure Protection, and Counter-terrorism on the National Security Council staff. This person, currently Richard Clarke, chairs the Critical Infrastructure Coordination Group (CICG), which serves as "the primary interagency working group for developing and implementing policy and for coordinating the federal government's own internal security measures." The CICG includes high-level agency representation (including the Sector Liaisons[13]), the National Economic Council, and all other relevant agencies. PDD-63 also established a National Information Assurance Council (NIAC) that includes private and local and state government representatives in the various sectors or infrastructures. PDD-63 called for a National Infrastructure Assurance Plan to provide an assessment of national needs in protecting the nation's infrastructure, as well as guidance in pursuing possible budgetary and legislative remedies. The Federal Bureau of Investigation (FBI) through the National Infrastructure Protection Center (NIPC) is given a lead role in

---

[10] Critical infrastructures are categorized as follows: information and communications; banking and finance; water supply; aviation, highways, mass transit pipeline, rail, and waterborne commerce; emergency, fire, and continuity of government services; public health services; electric power, oil and gas production, and storage.

[11] For a comprehensive and detailed overview of PDD-63, see Jack Moteff, *Critical Infrastructures: Background & Early Implementation of PDD-63*, CRS Report RL 30153, updated regularly.

[12] See [http://www.whitehouse.gov/media/pdf/npisp-fullreport-000112.pdf].

[13] Each of the critical infrastructures identified in footnote 7 are represented by a lead federal agency. For example, the Department of Treasury has the lead in banking and finance.

serving as an early warning center for information system attacks. There is also an extensive federal structure for dealing with terrorism.[14]

The Department of Defense and other military agencies play key roles in protecting sensitive information and infrastructure. Much of the responsibility for dealing with cyber threat and response policies is now consolidated under the Assistant Secretary of Defense C^3I (Command, Control, Communications, & Intelligence).[15] On October 1, 2000, U.S. Space Command at Peterson Air Force Base, Colorado, assumed operational responsibility for the CNA (Computer Network Attack) mission for the Department of Defense. U.S. Space Command now takes the military lead in defending DoD networks, as well as offensive information operations as an element of defending U.S. systems. CNA operations may also include counter-terrorism and support of U.S. military forces deployed in crisis or conflict.[16]

The services and the various defense agencies also contribute in various ways to the challenge of cyberwarfare. For example, the Joint Task Force – Computer Network Defense (JTF-CND) operations center opened in Virginia in August 1999. It was designed to serve as the focal point for defense of DoD computer systems.[17] Until that time, the various services and agencies had been left largely to determine how best to improve network and system security. The JTF-CND currently retains operational command for CND (Computer Network Defense) while U.S. Space Command is building a long-term, robust CND capability at Colorado Springs. In addition, some of the reserve forces, such as the Army Reserve, have created information operations centers trained and manned by so-called cyber-defense warriors.

Current Legal Framework. In addition to the various U.S. laws guiding the conduct of warfare in general and U.S. government conduct in cyberspace, a key document was produced by the Department of Defense that examined that range of treaties and international law as they might

---

[14] See [http://cns.miis.edu/research/cbw/response.htm].

[15] According to DoD Directive 5137.1, the Assistant Secretary is the principal staff assistant and advisor to the Secretary and Deputy Secretary of Defense for C^3I, information management (IM), information operations (IO), counter-intelligence (CI), and security countermeasures (SCM) matters, including warning, reconnaissance, and intelligence and intelligence-related activities conducted by the Department of Defense.

[16] New Release, September 29, 2000: [http://www.spacecom.af.mil/usspace/rel15-00.htm].

[17] Information about the Center can be found in IAnewsletter, Vol. 3, No. 4, pp. 10-15. Also, see [http://iac.dtic.mil/iatc].

pertain to the conduct of cyberwarfare.[18] This document is apparently playing an important role in guiding U.S. consideration of defensive and offensive operations in cyberspace. In essence, it makes several conclusions. First, it concludes there is little likelihood that the international community will soon generate a coherent body of information operations law. Second, it indicates there are no clear legal remedies or vehicles to address the type of information operations activities being considered by the United States. Third, and perhaps most relevant, the document recommends analyzing the various elements and circumstances of any particular planned operation or activity to determine how existing international legal principles are likely to apply.

Some have pointed out key legal issues that remain unresolved. These include, for example, the need for international agreements for expeditious pursuit of those violating the law, law enforcement needs in the conduct of electronic surveillance of those launching cyber attacks, possible legislation to encourage information sharing between the private sector and the government by protecting proprietary information and shielding sensitive information from FOIA (Freedom of Information Act) requests, and the establishment of clear and appropriate rules of engagement for cyber defense activities.[19] Some of these ideas are likely to generate controversy as national security interests are balanced against privacy concerns, for instance.

Recent Initiatives. In January 2000, President Clinton announced a 10-point $2 billion program designed to protect government computers and networks from cyber attacks. The President proposed spending this money to increase funding for research and development in identifying and addressing vulnerabilities, detecting cyber attacks, developing intelligence and law enforcement activities, and creating capabilities to respond and recover from cyber attacks. The White House had wanted the program to go into effect by the close of 2000, and for it to be fully operational by mid-2003. The Senate Judiciary Committee, Subcommittee on Technology, Terrorism, and Government Information held hearings in February 2000, but further action was not taken. Richard Clark (former National Security Council Coordinator for Security, Infrastructure Protection, and Counter-

---

[18] Department of Defense. Office of the General Counsel. *An Assessment of International Legal Issues in Information Operations.* May 1999.

[19] IAnewsletter, Vol. 3, No. 1.

terrorism) had expressed frustration on several occasions that Congress has neither acted on this proposal, nor similar Administration proposals designed to strengthen and fund U.S. security in cyberspace over the past two years.

Congressional Response, Reaction, and Activities

For the most part, the Executive Branch has taken the initiative thus far regarding information security and cyberwarfare issues. Congress regularly supports funding for a wide range of activities that are designed to protect government information systems and data. Much of this funding goes for programs that can be considered information assurance. These efforts are found in virtually every federal agency and are simply part of the normal responsibilities of government agencies. An accurate account of total annual funding for these efforts is not available.

Congress also regularly supports a broad range of national security programs that are in various ways related to information assurance and information operations. Many of these are found in the services, and throughout the various defense agencies. Although, requested, the Defense Department could not provide us with a budget estimate for these programs. In perhaps large part, this is because there remains some lack of consensus as to what constitutes information operations or cyberwarfare activities within the Defense Department (even though a DoD definition exists). In addition, many of the tasks that might be considered information operations are part of what the military ordinarily does. Nonetheless, neither the Defense Department nor Congress has fully separated out these activities. This makes it difficult therefore to determine whether the overall funding is adequate or redundant, or even effective.

Some in Congress introduced relevant legislation this year. For instance, in March 2000, Rep. Jim Saxton introduced H.Con.Res. 282, which designates cyberterrorism an emerging national security threat. The bill calls for federal and private sector partnership, a revised legal framework for dealing with the problem, and a new federal study to assess the threat posed by cyberterrorism. The bill was referred to the House Judiciary (subcommittee on Crime) and Commerce (subcommittee on Telecommunications, Trade, and Consumer Protection) committees on March 15, 2000 where it remains. In April 2000, Sen. Orrin Hatch introduced S.2448 (Internet Integrity and Critical Infrastructure Protection Act of 2000). It was referred to the Senate Judiciary Committee on April 13,

2000, where it remained until October 5, 2000 when it was placed on the Senate Legislative Calendar.

Congress has expressed concern in other ways also. Rep. Stephen Horn, for instance, gave poor grades to the various Executive Branch agencies for efforts to strengthen and secure government networks.[20] Rep. Curt Weldon has charged the Administration with neglecting the problem of cyberterrorism and cyber threats to the United States.[21]

SELECTED FOREIGN VIEWS AND ACTIVITIES

This section is not intended to be comprehensive, but rather illustrative of some of the major actors in the cyberwarfare arena. In general, some hold views comparable to the United States, including the UK, Germany, and NATO. France, however, may be an exception, because many observers have concluded that the French may see a legitimate role for economic cyberwarfare in the pursuit of national objectives. Russian rhetoric portrays cyberwarfare as an act of war for which any response, conventional or with weapons of mass destruction, is deemed justified. China sees cyberwarfare as a legitimate for of asymmetrical warfare and is preparing cadres of computer professionals for this task. These views re-examined in more detail below.

Russia

Many Russians argue that the danger of cyberwarfare ranks second only to that of nuclear war. More than one senior Russian military officer has supported the notion that:

> From a military point of view, the use of Information
> Warfare against Russia or its armed forces will

---

[20] See Horn Releases First-Ever Government-Wide Computer Security Evaluation. News Release. House Subcommittee on Government Management, Information, and Technology. September 11, 2000. "Overall, the government earned an average grade of 'D-'. More than one-quarter of the 24 major federal agencies received a failing 'F'.

[21] Rep. Curt Weldon made these remarks in a Keystone address at the InfoWarCon 2000 Convention, September 12, 2000, Washington, DC.

categorically not be considered a non-military phase of a
conflict whether there were casualties or not...considering
the possible catastrophic use of strategic information
warfare means by an enemy, whether on economic or state
command and control systems, or on the combat potential
of the armed forces...Russia retains the right to use
nuclear weapons first against the means and forces of
information warfare, and then against the aggressor state
itself.[22]

Other Russians see a military role for cyberwarfare activities, where the
goal is for competing sides to gain and hold information advantages over the
other. This is accomplished by using specific information technology
capabilities to affect an adversary's information systems, decision-making
processes, command and control system, and even populace.[23] Some
Russians believe that after conflict begins, "combat viruses and other
information related weapons can be used as powerful force multipliers."

More recently, on September 12, 2000, Russian President Vladimir
Putin adopted the Russian Information Security Doctrine, which had been
approved earlier at the June 23 meeting of the Russian Security Council.
The new doctrine ostensibly provides the government with an enhanced
legal framework for dealing with computer crime and assuring security in
cyberspace. In another sense, this represents a partial attempt by Russia to
deal with cyber threats it too faces from foreign and domestic sources.

People's Republic of China (PRC)

China is moving aggressively toward incorporating cyberwarfare into its
military lexicon, organization, training, and doctrine. In fact, if a Revolution
in Military Affairs (RMA) is defined as a significant change in technology

---

[22] V.I.Tsymbal, "Knotseptsiya 'Informatsionnoy voyny'", (Concept of Information
Warfare), speech given at the Russian-U.S. conference on "Evolving post Cold
War National Security Issues," Moscow 12-14 Sept., 1995 p. 7. Cited in Col.
Timothy Thomas, "Russian Views on Information-Based Warfare."
[http://call.army.mil/call/fmso/fmsopubs/issues/rusvuiw.htm.]. Paper published
in a special issue of *Airpower Journal,* July 1996.

[23] Lester W. Grau and Timothy L. Thomas. "A Russian View of Future War: Theory
and Direction," *The Journal of Slavic Military Studies.* Issue 9.3 (September
1996), pp. 501-518.

taken advantage of by comparable changes in military training, organization, and doctrine, then perhaps China of all nations is experiencing a true RMA in cyberspace.

The Chinese concept of cyberwarfare incorporates unique Chinese views of warfare based around the People's War concept (modern) and the 36 Stratagems (ancient). Both are indigenous views of how to wage war at the strategic, operational, and tactical level. China also is heavily influenced by Marxist-Leninist ideology regarding warfare. Much of its approach has to do with an emphasis on deception, knowledge-style war, and seeking asymmetrical advantages over an adversary. Cyberwarfare is seen as a "transformation from the mechanized warfare of the industrial age to ...a war of decisions and control, a war of knowledge, and a war of intellect."[24]

China is pursuing the concept of a Net Force (battalion size), which would consist of a strong reserve force of computer experts trained at a number of universities, academies, and training centers. Several large annual training exercises have already taken place since 1997. The Chinese have placed significant emphasis on training younger persons for these tasks.

United Kingdom (UK)

The UK view toward cyberwarfare is similar to that of the United States. Basically, it notes that information warfare refers to actions affecting others' information systems while defending one's own systems in support of national objectives.[25] Furthermore, the UK uses a legal framework based around a number of existing laws it believes largely can be applied to cyberspace activities.[26] This suggests that the UK views cyber attacks

---

[24] Military Strategic Research Center, Beijing, May 1996.

[25] In June 2000, the UK defined IW as "integrated actions undertaken to influence decision makers in support of political and military objectives by affecting others information, information based processes, C2 (command & control), systems, and CIS (critical infrastructure systems) while exploiting and protecting one's own information and/or information systems."

[26] These include the: Computer Misuse Act (1990), Telecommunications Act (1984). Telecommunications (Fraud) Act 1987, Obscene Publications Act (1959 and 1964), Protection of Children Act (1978), Criminal Justice Act (1988), Criminal Justice and Public Order Act (1994), Data Protection Acts (1984 and 1998),

against individuals and corporations as civil and criminal issues that can be handled accordingly. More recently, the Regulation of Investigatory Powers Act 2000 (RIP), would allow the UK government to intercept and read e-mail, and require decryption of personal files on demand. The UK government says RIP puts "intrusive investigative techniques on a statutory footing for the very first time; provides new powers to help combat the threat posed by rising criminal use of strong encryption; and ensures that there is independent oversight of the powers in the Act."[27]

Germany

For the most part, the German perspective toward cyberwarfare is comparable to that of the United States and the UK.[28] It recognizes a legitimate role for offensive and defensive information warfare in pursuit of national objectives. Germany tends to be somewhat more systematic than the United States, however. For purposes of thinking about cyber threats and cyber responses, nation states are considered separately from non-state actors (such as political activists, international organizations, and the media), criminals (organized crime, hackers, etc.), and individual actors (including religious fanatics and special forces).

In two ways, however, German views toward information warfare may differ. Germany may include management of the media as an element of information warfare. In addition, Germany may be weighing a rationale for economic cyberwarfare similar to the French (see below). This may be due to several reasons: Germany has assessed the potential for economic damage that can be done to German business and economy; Germany may have experienced significant economic losses to France over a case involving industrial espionage in cyberspace; and Germany may be seeking ways to mitigate the consequences of potential cyber attacks.

Theft Acts (1968 and 1978), Forgery and Counterfeiting Act (1981), Copyright Design and Patents Act (1988), and Interception of Communications Act (1985).
[27] [http://www.homeoffice.gov.uk/ripa/ripact.htm].
[28] The German section is taken largely from a paper presented by Andy Jones, The European Perspective, at the InfoWarCon 2000 Convention, September 11, 2000, Washington, DC. Much of his analysis was taken from French and German language Web sites.

North Atlantic Treaty Organization (NATO)

Reportedly, there is a classified NATO definition of information warfare, but it is not publicly available. The development of such a definition is noteworthy given that at a NATO conference in early 2000, 17 different descriptions or definitions of IW were being used by the individual delegate countries. Generally, however, the NATO definition is believed to be compatible with the U.S. perspective.

France

The French apparently view cyberwarfare as having two main elements: military and economic (or civil).[29] The military concept envisions a somewhat limited role for cyberwarfare activities. Their military concept sees cyberwarfare activities taking place largely in the context of low intensity conflict or operations other than war, undertaken generally within the framework of NATO and the United Nations (and often under the control of the United States). In this context, allies are not considered adversaries.

In contrast, the economic or civil concept includes a wider range of potential cyberwarfare applications. The French view seems to assume a much broader and deeper basis for conflict in the economic sphere; economic peace does not exist as much as an environment in which competitors pursue zero-sum market advantages. The French do not see themselves bound by NATO, UN, or U.S. approval. Their perspective toward allows for one to be both an ally and an adversary at the same time. The French even have an economic school for information warfare.[30]

France may also have a different perspective toward monitoring its citizens in cyberspace. Reports have surfaced that the French have their own version of Echelon (reportedly a U.S. effort – not officially verified – aimed at intercepting virtually all private global communications).[31] Frenchelon, as

---

[29] See [http://www.infoguerre.com] (in French).
[30] See[http://www.ege.eslsca.fr] (in French).
[31] See Richard Best. *Project Echelon: U.S. Electronic Surveillance Efforts.* CRS Report RS20444,
March 2, 2000.

some have called it, reportedly is used to monitor and analyze French communications, especially in the Paris region.[32]

Non-State Actors

There is considerable evidence that some non-state actors and anti-government forces use cyberspace as another tool to wage their fight against various nations. For example, Mexico's Zapitista movement uses the World Wide Web to elicit support for its cause ([http://www.ezln.org]). Afghanistan's Taliban militia – a movement that controls most of Afghanistan – maintains a site with a range of material and even solicits contributions from abroad ([http://www.afghan-ie.com]). Similarly, there is an Internet site Basque National Liberation Movement (a separatist movement in the region between Spain and France ([http://theimageworks.com/eta.com/default.htm]).

CYBERTERRORISM

There appears to be reasonable evidence available that terrorist organizations use cyberspace to conduct the business of terrorism. Terrorists use the Internet and the World Wide Web to communicate with each other, recruit members, gather intelligence, raise money legally and illegally, organize and coordinate activities, obtain illegal passports and visas, and distribute propaganda. For instance:

- Some Afghan-based terrorists, such as Osama bin-Laden, reportedly have computers, communications equipment, and large data storage disks for their operations.[33]
- Hamas, a Middle Eastern terrorist organization, reportedly uses Internet chat rooms and e-mail to plan and coordinate operations in Gaza, the West Bank, and Lebanon.[34]

---

[32]   "Frenchelon, the Large Ears Made in France." See [http://www.zdnet.fr/actu/tech/secu/a0014768.html].

[33] Afghanistan, Saudi Arabia, " Editor's Journey to Meet Bin-Laden Described, " London al-Quds al-'Arabi, FBIS-TOT-97-003-L, November 27, 1996, p. 4.

[34] Israel: U.S. Hamas Activists Use Internet to Send Attack Threats," Tel Aviv IDF Radio, FBIS-TOT-97-001-L, October 13, 1996.

- Hizballah, another Middle Eastern group, manages several Internet Web sites for propaganda purposes ([http://www.hizbollah.org/]), to describe attacks against Israel ([http://www.moqawama.org/]), and one for news and information ([http://www.almanar.com.lb/]).
- Government computers reportedly were crashed by terrorist groups during elections in Indonesia, Sri Lanka, and Mexico.[35]
- Irish Republican Army (IRA) supporters reportedly leaked sensitive details on British army bases in Northern Ireland on the Internet. Sinn Fein also maintains a web site ([http://sinnfein.ie/]).

But is this cyberterrorism? If terrorism is defined as an act of violence designed to achieve political objectives, do these activities constitute act of violence? Should these types of activities more accurately be described as techno-terrorism, the terrorist's use of technology, satellite communications, e-mail, and the Internet in their business? Some observers express concern that terrorists want to bring down the Internet. But if terrorists rely on the Internet, why would they want to bring it down? Others, in and out of government, express concern about terrorists targeting power and communications grids, for example. But Richard Clarke (National Security Council Coordinator for Security, Infrastructure Protection, and Counter-terrorism), has said several times it does not appear that terrorist groups actually are planning to use the Internet for these kinds of activities.

So is cyberspace another tool to be exploited by terrorists, and does U.S. and western reliance on information systems and cyberspace represent a significant vulnerability awaiting terrorist attack? Currently, there does not appear to be a consensus answer, although most would agree that attention and resources should be devoted to this issue given the high stakes.

CHALLENGES AND ISSUES FOR CONGRESS

Cyberwarfare is an emerging issue for national interest. At this point, however, a coherent consensus strategy is lacking. Should cyber threats be considered primarily a domestic or civil responsibility for law enforcement

---

[35] See [http://www.inforwar.com/class_3/99/class3_071699b_j.shtml].

and the judicial system, or are cyber threats to U.S. infrastructure a national security responsibility? In the past, responsibilities were more easily managed because geography often represented obstacles to adversaries. Geography is much less an obstacle today.

Another reason a coherent consensus approach may be lacking is due to the complexity and diversity of the topic and the absence of technological means to determine unambiguously and in real time where computer or network attacks are coming from. Without an extensive commitment of time and resources, cyber attacks are difficult to trace with a high degree of confidence.

But without clear national guidance, issues such as appropriate organization, responsibility, and funding will likely remain problematic. In light of the fact that the U.S. response to information capabilities is still evolving, Congress may seek to determine the scope of executive branch spending for cyberwarfare-related activities, and further examine whether such levels are sufficient, coordinated, or duplicative. The government's conceptual and organizational approach toward cyberwarfare may be of legislative interest. Congress may also weigh in on whether an individual or some agency should have primacy in issues dealing with cyberwarfare.

APPENDIX: TERMS & DEFINITIONS

For ease of discussion, **cyberwarfare** in this report is used broadly to mean warfare waged in cyberspace. It can include *defending* information and computer networks, *deterring* information attacks, as well as *denying* an adversary's ability to do the same. It can include *offensive* information operations mounted against an adversary, or even *dominating* information on the battlefield. Other, more technical and precise terms are indicated below for reference.

Information Warfare (IW) "it involves actions taken to achieve information superiority by affecting adversary information, information-based processes, information systems, and computer-based networks while defending one's own information, information-based processes, information systems, and computer-based networks." (Department of Defense Directive 3600.1) IW is further defined as Information Operations conducted during time of crisis or conflict to achieve or promote specific objectives over a specific adversary or adversaries. (IATAC TR-97-002).

Note that some key observers outside of government have defined IW to include personal and corporate warfare (attacks on individuals or companies by other individuals or companies).[36] Some Europeans tend to share this perspective as well. Critics charge that "warfare" is not focused on individuals or commercial organizations. They argue that attacks against individuals are civil or criminal litigation issues, while attacks against corporations by other companies are acts of industrial espionage, although they acknowledge that an attack by a government or terrorist group may in fact be Information Warfare.

Special Information Operations (SIO) are information operations that by their sensitive nature, due to their potential effect or impact, security requirements, or risk to national security of the United States, require a special review and approval process. (Department of Defense Directive 3600.1)

Information Superiority is "that degree of dominance in the information domain which permits the conduct of operations without effective opposition." (Department of Defense Directive 3600.1) It is the capability to collect, process, and disseminate an uninterrupted flow of information while exploiting or denying an adversary's ability to do the same.

Information Assurance (IA) is "Information Operations that protect and defend information systems by ensuring their availability, integrity, authentication, confidentiality and non-repudiation. This includes providing for restoration of information systems by incorporating protection, detection and reaction capabilities." (Department of Defense Directive 3600.1)

- **IA Authentication** are security measures "designed to establish the validity of a transmission, message, or originator, or a mean[s] of verifying an individual's authorization to receive specific categories of information." (National Telecommunications Information Systems Security Instructions – NSTISSI – 4009)
- **IA Availability** refers to timely, reliable access to data and information services for authorized users. (NSTISSI – 4009)

---

[36] See Winn Schwartau, *Information Warfare: Cyberterrorism: Protecting Your Personal Security in the Electronic Age.* New York, NE: Thunder's Mouth Press, 1994, pp. 473-587.

- **IA Confidentiality** is assurance that information is not disclosed to unauthorized persons, processes, or devices. (NSTISSI – 4009)
- **IA Integrity** is protection against unauthorized modification or destruction of information. (NSTISSI – 4009)
- **IA Nonrepudiation** is assurance that the end user of data is provided with proof of delivery and the recipient is provided with proof of the sender's identity, so neither can subsequently deny having processed the data. (NSTISSI – 4009)

Computer Network Attack (CNA) are operations designed to disrupt, deny, degrade, or destroy information resident in computers and computer networks, or the computers or networks themselves. (Department of Defense Directive 3600.1)

Electronic Warfare (EW) is defined as "any military action involving the use of electromagnetic and directed energy to control the electromagnetic spectrum or to attack any enemy." (Chairman, Joint Chiefs of Staff MOP 6). It is a well-established component of contemporary combat not necessarily involved with cyberspace.

TERRORISM, THE FUTURE, AND U.S. FOREIGN POLICY

Raphael F. Perl

MOST RECENT DEVELOPMENTS

Investigations continue to determine culpability for the October 12, 2000 attack on U.S.S. Cole, a navy destroyer refueling in the Yemen's seaport of Aden. Seventeen American servicemen were killed and 39 injured in the explosion which seriously damaged the ship with the cost of repairs estimated at $240 million. The attack is believed to be the work of radical Islamic militants. Meanwhile, Administration officials are weighing response options should culpability lead to Osama Bin Laden or other clearly identifiable private groups or state sponsors.

In related developments, Administration officials are preparing briefing material on international terrorism for presidential transition team members. Suggested initiatives include: (1) a regional initiative to isolate Afghanistan; (2) enhanced policy focus on sanctions against Iran for their active support of Mid-east terrorist groups and operations; and (3) elevating the State Department's Counter-Terrorism Office to full "Bureau" (Assistant Secretary) status.

BACKGROUND AND ANALYSIS

In recent years, terrorism has been primarily viewed as an international and foreign policy issue. Numerous acts of state-sponsored terrorists and of foreign-based groups have given support to this notion. While U.S. policies, citizens and interests are prime targets for international terrorism – in 1999 approximately 52%, up from 40% in 1998, of all terrorist incidents worldwide were committed against U.S. citizens or property according to the U.S. Department of State – the vast majority of those acts took place on foreign soil. Although terrorism may be internationally motivated, financed, supported or planned, on the receiving end all terrorism is local. Thus, U.S. public perception of terrorism as primarily an overseas issue may be changing with the bombings of the Trade Center in New York and the Federal Building in Oklahoma City. The predominant method of attack during 1999 was bombing (roughly one-half); the most common targets were business related.

On May 1, 2000, the Department of State released its Patterns of Global Terrorism report (*Patterns* 1999). In 1999, casualties associated with terrorism worldwide were significantly down from 1998 data. The report indicates that worldwide deaths from terrorist incidents are down roughly threefold from 1998 (from 741 to 233) and the number of wounded was down roughly eightfold from 5,952 to 706. In terms of deaths by region, Asia ranked first; Africa, second; and the Middle East, third. In terms of wounded by region, Asia ranked first, Africa, second, and the Middle East, third as well. In 1998, Africa was highest in both the number of dead and wounded by terrorism; Asia was in second place. In 1999, the number of attacks rose in all regions of the world except the Middle East.

Both timing and target selection by terrorist groups has produced significant political and economic impact on phenomena such as the Middle East peace process and tourism in nations such as Egypt. Some analysts have expressed concern that radical Islamic groups may seek to exploit economic and political instabilities in Saudi Arabia. Other potential target nations of such groups include Algeria, Bahrain, Egypt, India, Jordan, Turkey, and Pakistan. *Patterns 1999* suggests that a decline in state sponsorship of terrorism has moved terrorism eastward from Libya, Syria, and Lebanon to South Asia. The result: more U.S. policy focus on Osama bin Laden and the alliance of groups operating out of Afghanistan with the acquiescence of the Taliban. A heavy area of focus remains the ability of terrorists to raise funds through non-state sources, often through charitable contributions, kidnapping, and drug trafficking.

Patterns 1999 cited North Korea, Cuba, and Syria as possible candidates for removal from the list of state sponsors of terrorism. Iran, despite political changes in 1999, is again listed as the most active state sponsor of international terrorism. Iran and Syria were cited for supporting regional terrorist groups, and Lebanon was cited as a key safe haven. Concern was expressed by Russia and Chechnya's neighbors that increased radicalization of Islamist populations would encourage violence and spread instability elsewhere in Russia and beyond. Though not added to the list, Afghanistan and Pakistan were singled out as major sites of terrorist activity. The bombings of U.S. Embassies in East Africa, of the N.Y. World Trade Center, and of the Jewish cultural center in Buenos Aires may indicate a trend to inflict higher casualties on what are generally less protected civilian targets. It appears that state-sponsored terrorism is decreasing significantly as, in a post-Cold War era, groups find it harder to obtain sponsors and rogue states are less willing to risk exposure to broad based and severe international sanctions. In this environment, access to private sources of funding for terrorist enterprises becomes critical.

International terrorism is recognized as a threat to U.S. foreign and domestic security; it also undermines a broad range of U.S. foreign policy goals. Terrorism erodes international stability, a major foreign and economic policy objective for the United States. Terrorist groups often seek to destabilize or overthrow governments, sometimes democratically elected – or friendly – government, and such groups often draw their support from public discontent over the perceived inability of governments to deliver peace, security, and economic prosperity. Efforts by governments to enhance national or regional economic development and stability may become the object of particularly virulent attack. In this regard, and because of their avowed goals to overthrow secular regimes in countries with large Muslim populations, extremist Islamic fundamentalist groups, and Iran's support for such groups, are seen as a major threat to U.S. foreign policy goals and objectives.

DEFINITIONS

There is no universally accepted definition of international terrorism. One definition widely used in U.S. government circles, and incorporated into law, defines "international terrorism" as terrorism involving the citizens or property of more than one country. Terrorism is broadly defined as politically motivated violence perpetrated against noncombatant targets by sub national groups or clandestine agents. A "terrorist group" is defined as a group which practices or which has significant subgroups which practice terrorism (22 U.S.C. 2656f). One potential shortfall of this traditional approach is its focus on groups and group members and exclusion of individual (non-group organized) terrorist activity which has recently risen in frequency and visibility. Another possible weakness of these standard definitions is the criteria of violence in a traditional form. Analysts pointing to "virus" sabotage incidents warn that terrorists acts could include more sophisticated forms of destruction and extortion such as disabling a national infrastructure by penetrating vital computer software.

Current definitions of terrorism all share one common element: politically motivated behavior. Such definitions do not include violence for financial profit or religious motivation. The rapid growth of transnational criminal organizations and the growing range and scale of such operations could well result in their use of violence to achieve objectives with financial profit as the driving motivation. Thus, although the basic assumption today is that all terrorist acts are politically motivated, some are driven by other factors, and this number may grow in light of expanding international criminal activity and an increasing number of extremist acts carried out in the name of religious and cultural causes. A new approach might focus more on defining terrorist acts, giving less emphasis to the motivation behind the acts.

U.S. POLICY RESPONSE

Framework

Past administrations have employed a range of options to combat international terrorism, from diplomacy and international cooperation and constructive engagement to economic sanctions, covert action, protective security measures and military force. The application of sanctions is one of the most frequently used tools of U.S. policymakers. Governments supporting international terrorism (as defined by the Department of State) are prohibited from receiving U.S. economic and military assistance. Export of munitions to such countries is foreclosed; restrictions are imposed on exports of "dual use" equipment such as aircraft and trucks.

Throughout successive administrations, U.S. policy as publicly stated has remained: no concessions to terrorists, the U.S. government will not pay ransoms, release prisoners, change its policies, nor agree to other acts that might encourage additional terrorism. Practice, however, has not always been so pure. Recent U.S. and Israeli overtures to the PLO, and recent U.S.

and British approaches to the IRA clearly appear to reflect some change in approach as such groups begin to moderate their behavior.

Most experts agree that the most effective way to fight terrorism is to gather as much intelligence as possible; disrupt terrorist plans and organizations before they act; and organize multinational cooperation against terrorists and countries that support them. The U.N.'s role in mandating sanctions against Libya for its responsibility in the 1988 Pan Am 103 bombing was significant as the first instance when the world community imposed sanctions against a country in response to its complicity in an act of terrorism. Several factors made the action possible. First, terrorism has touched many more countries in recent years, forcing governments to put aside parochial interests. (Citizens from over 30 countries have reportedly died in Libyan-sponsored bombings.) Second, the end of the Cold War has contributed to increased international cooperation against terrorism. And third, U.S. determination to punish terrorist countries, by military force in some instances, once their complicity was established, was a major factor spurring other countries to join U.N.-sponsored action.

In the past, governments have often preferred to handle terrorism as a national problem without outside interference. Some governments were also wary of getting involved in others battles and possibly attracting additional terrorism in the form of reprisals. Others were reluctant to join in sanctions if their own trade interests might be damaged or they sympathized with the perpetrators' cause. Finally, there is the persistent problem of extraditing terrorists without abandoning the long-held principle of asylum for persons fleeing persecution for legitimate political or other activity.

Dilemmas

In their desire to combat terrorism in a modern political context, nations often face conflicting goals and courses of action: (1) providing security from terrorist acts, i.e. limiting the freedom if individual terrorists, terrorists groups, and support networks to operate unimpeded in a relative unregulated environment versus (2) maximizing individual freedoms, democracy, and human rights. Efforts to combat terrorism are complicated by a global trend towards deregulation, open borders, and expanded commerce. Particularly in democracies such as the United States, the constitutional limits within which policy must operate are often seen to conflict directly with a desire to secure the lives of citizens against terrorist activity more effectively.

Another dilemma for policymakers is the need to identify the perpetrators of particular terrorist acts and those who train, fund, or otherwise support or sponsor them. Moreover, as the international community increasingly demonstrates its ability to unite and apply sanctions against rogue states, states will become less likely to overtly support terrorist groups or engage in state sponsored terrorism.

Today a non-standard brand of terrorist may be emerging: individuals who do not work for any established terrorist organization and who are apparently not agents of any state sponsor. The worldwide threat of such individual or "boutique" terrorism, or that of "spontaneous" terrorist activity such as the bombing of bookstores in the United States after Ayatollah Khomeini's death edict against Salman Rushdie, appears to be on the increase. Thus, one likely profile for the terrorist of the 21st century may well be a private individual not affiliated with any established group. Another profile might be a group-affiliated individual acting independent of the group, but drawing on other similarly minded individuals for support. Because U.S. international counter-terrorism policy framework is sanctions-oriented, and has traditionally sought to pin responsibility on state-sponsors, some policy realignment may be required.

Another problem surfacing in the wake of the number of incidents associated with Islamic fundamentalist groups is how to condemn and combat such terrorist activity, and the extreme and violent ideology of specific radical groups, without appearing to be anti-Islamic in general. A desire to punish a state for supporting international terrorism may also be subject to conflicting foreign policy objectives.

Policy Tools

The U.S. government has employed a wide array of policy tools to combat international terrorism, from diplomacy and international cooperation and constructive engagement to economic sanctions, covert action, protective security measures, and military force.

Diplomacy/Constructive Engagement. Most responses to international terrorism involve use of diplomacy in some form as governments seek cooperation to apply pressure on terrorists. One such initiative was the active U.S. role taken in the March 1996 Sharm al-Sheikh peacemaker/anti-terrorism summit. Another is the ongoing U.S. effort to get Japan and major European nations to join in U.S. trade and economic sanctions against Iran. Some argue that diplomacy holds little hope of success against determined terrorists or the countries that support them. However, diplomatic measures are least likely to widen the conflict and therefore are usually tried first.

In incidents of international terrorism by sub national groups, implementing a policy response of constructive engagement is complicated by the lack of existing channels and mutually accepted rules of conduct between governmental entities and the group in question. In some instances, as was the case with the PLO, legislation may specifically prohibit official contact with a terrorist organization or its members. Increasingly, however, governments appear to be pursuing policies which involve verbal contact with terrorist groups or their representatives.

The media remain powerful forces in confrontations between terrorists and governments. Appealing to, and influencing, public opinion may impact not only the actions of governments but also those of groups engaged in terrorist acts. From the terrorist perspective, media coverage is an important measure of the success of a terrorist act or campaign. And in hostage type incidents, where the media may provide the only independent means a terrorist has of knowing the chain of events set in motion, coverage can complicate rescue efforts. Governments can use the media in an effort to arouse world opinion against the country or group using terrorist tactics. Public diplomacy and the media can be used to mobilize public opinion in other countries to pressure government to take action against terrorism. An example would be to mobilize the tourist industry to pressure governments into participating in sanctions against a terrorist state.

Economic Sanctions. In the past, use of economic sanctions was usually predicated upon identification of a nation as an active supporter or sponsor of international terrorism. On August 20, 1998, President Clinton signed an executive order freezing assets owned by Saudi-born Islamic terrorist leader Osama bin Laden, specific associates, and their self-proclaimed Islamic Army Organization, and prohibiting U.S. individuals and firms from doing business with them. Previously, the Clinton Administration had frozen the assets of 12 alleged Middle East terrorist organizations and 18 individuals associated with those organizations. On October 8, 1997, the State Department released a list of 30 foreign terrorist organizations. As of October 1999, the number of organizations on this list stood at 28. The 1996 Antiterrorism and Effective Death Penalty Act makes it a crime to provide support to these organizations, and their members shall be denied entry visas into the United States.

On August 10, 1999, the United States froze the assets of Afghanistan's national airline under sanctions designed to punish the Taliban movement for harboring bin Laden. Apprehension of bin Laden remains a publicly announced top priority for the U.S. counter-terrorism community, despite suggestions from some that such policy focus overstates his importance, aids his recruitment efforts, neglects other foreign policy and national security priorities, and diverts resources from other counter-terrorism areas where they are badly needed. In related developments, on July 6, 1999, the United States banned trade with parts of Afghanistan controlled by the Taliban.

Economic sanctions fall into six categories: restrictions on trading, technology transfer, foreign assistance, export credits and guarantees, foreign exchange and capital transactions, and economic access. Sanctions may include a total or partial trade embargo, embargo on financial transactions, suspension of foreign aid, restrictions on aircraft or ship traffic, or abrogation of a friendship, commerce, and navigation treaty. Sanctions usually require the cooperation of other countries to make them effective, and such cooperation is not always forthcoming.

The President has a variety of laws at this disposal, but the broadest in its potential scope is the International Emergency Economic Powers Act. The Act permits imposition of restrictions on economic relations once the President has declared a national emergency because of a threat to the U.S. national security, foreign policy, or economy. While the sanctions authorized must deal directly with the threat responsible for the emergency, the President can regulate imports, exports, and all types of financial transactions, such as the transfer of funds, foreign exchange, credit, and securities, between the United States and the country in question. Specific authority for the Libyan trade embargo is in Section 503 of the International Trade and Security Act of 1985, while Section 505 of the Act authorizes the banning of imports of goods and services from any country supporting terrorism.

Other major laws that can be used against countries sponsoring terrorism are the Export Administration Act, Arms Export Control act, foreign assistance legislation. The Export Administration Act (Section 6(j)) allows the President to regulate export of dual use technology and prohibit or curtail the export of critical technology or other technological data. U.S. sales of technology, particularly high technology processes, have been considerable, and sales restrictions or prohibitions are known to have put pressure on states reluctant to control terrorism. Under this Act, exports of various sensitive articles to terrorism-list states are strictly controlled or prohibited because of their support of terrorism. The Arms Export Control Act authorizes the President to restrict the sale of defense articles and restrict or suspend defense services to states fostering terrorism. Foreign assistance authorization and appropriations acts deny foreign aid to countries supporting terrorism and require the U.S. to vote against loans to such countries in the multilateral developments banks. Country specific export control restrictions on munitions list items and dual use equipment apply to Iraq and Iran and are found in the Iraq Sanctions Act (Section 586 of P.L. 101-513). More recently, Executive Orders 12957 and 12959 prohibit U.S. development of Iran's oil industry and U.S. exports to and imports from Iran, as well as third country reexport of U.S. products to the Islamic Republic. P.L. 104-172, the 1996 Iran Oil Sanction's Act, prohibits U.S. trade with companies that invest more than $40 million in Iran's or Libya's petroleum development, or with companies not complying with U.N. mandated embargoes on sales of oil equipment to Libya. On March 17, 2000, Secretary of State Albright announced suspension of a ban on imports of Iranian pistachio nuts, caviar, and carpets – a move seen as a gesture to Iranian reformers and their supporters.

P.L. 104-132 prohibits the sale of arms to any country the President certifies is not cooperating fully with U.S. anti-terrorism efforts. The seven terrorist list countries and Afghanistan are currently on this list. Sections 325 and 326 of this law also require that aid be withheld to any country providing lethal military aid to countries on the terrorism list.

On July 6, 1999, President Clinton issued an executive order imposing sanctions against the Taliban and on October 15, 1999, the U.N. Security Council unanimously adopted a resolution imposing limited sanctions against the Taliban. The Council demanded that the Taliban turn over alleged Saudi terrorist suspect Osama bin Laden to a country where he will be effectively brought to justice. Sanctions called for include (1) denying aircraft landing and takeoffs to and from Taliban controlled territory, and (2) freezing funds and financials resources from Taliban owned or controlled undertakings.

The United States can suspend airline service to and from a nation or deny entry to terrorists and their supporters. In 1978, the United States joined with West Germany, Canada, Britain, France, Italy, and Japan in declaring a willingness to suspend commercial airline service between any of those countries and any country harboring hijackers. Recently, efforts have been made to sanction third-party countries for trading with an already sanctioned country.

Covert Action. Intelligence gathering, infiltration or terrorist groups and military operations involve a variety of clandestine or so-called "covert" activities. Much of this activity is of a passive monitoring nature. A more active form of covert activity occurs during events such as a hostage crisis or hijacking when a foreign country may quietly request advice, equipment or technical support during the conduct of operations, with no public credit to be given the providing country.

Some nations have periodically gone beyond monitoring or covert support activities and resorted to unconventional methods beyond their territory for the express purpose of neutralizing individual terrorists and/or thwarting preplanned attacks. Examples of activities might run the gamut from intercepting or sabotaging delivery of funding or weapons to the terrorist group to seizing and transporting a wanted terrorist to stand trial for assassination or murder. Arguably, such activity might be justified as preemptive self-defense under Article 51 of the U.N. charter. On the other hand, it could be argued that such actions violate customary international law. Nevertheless, a July 1989 memorandum by the Department of Justice's Office of Legal Counsel advises that the President has the authority to violate customary international law and can delegate such authority to the Attorney General level, should the national interest so require.

Assassination is specifically prohibited by U.S. Executive Order (most recently, E.O. 12333), but bringing of wanted criminals to the United States for trial is not. There exists an established U.S. legal doctrine that allows an individual's trial to proceed regardless of whether he is forcefully abducted from another country, or from international waters or airspace. For example, Fawaz Yunis, a Lebanese who participated in the 1985 hijacking of a Jordanian airliner with two Americans among its 70 passengers, was lured aboard a yacht in international waters off the coast of Cyprus in 1987 by federal agents, flown to the United States for trial, and convicted.

Experts warn that bringing persons residing abroad to U.S. justice by means other than extradition or mutual agreement with the host country, i.e., by abduction and their surreptitious transportation, can vastly complicate U.S. foreign relations, perhaps jeopardizing interests far more important than "justice," deterrence, and the prosecution of a single individual. For example, the abduction of a Mexican national in 1990 to stand trial in Los Angeles on charges relating to torture and death of a DEA agent led to vehement protests from the government of Mexico, a government subsequently plagued with evidence of high level drug related corruption. Subsequently, in November 1994, the two countries signed a treaty to Prohibit Trans-border Abductions. Notwithstanding the unpopularity of such abductions in nations that fail to apprehend and prosecute those accused, the "rendering" of such wanted criminals to U.S. courts is permitted under limited circumstances by a January 1993 Presidential Decision Directive issued under the Bush Administration, and reaffirmed by President Clinton. Such conduct, however, raises prospects of other nations using similar tactics against U.S. citizens.

Although conventional explosives – specifically car bombs – appear to be the terrorism weapon of choice, the world is increasingly moving into an era in which terrorists may gain access to nuclear, chemical or biological weaponry. Faced with the potential of more frequent incidents and higher conventional casualty levels, or a nuclear or biological holocaust, nations may be more prone to consider covert operations designed to neutralize such threats.

Rewards for Information Program. Money is a powerful motivator. Rewards for information have been instrumental in Italy in destroying the Red Brigades and in Colombia in apprehending drug cartel leaders. A State Department program is in place, supplemented by the aviation industry, offering rewards of up to $4 million to anyone providing information that would prevent or resolve an act of international terrorism against U.S. citizens or U.S. property, or that leads to the arrest or conviction of terrorist criminals involved in such acts. This program was at least partly responsible for the arrest of the Unabomber, of Ramzi Ahmed Yousef, the man accused of masterminding the World Trade Center bombing, and of the CIA personnel shooter, Mir Amal Kansi. The program was established by the 1984 Act to Combat International Terrorism (P.L. 98-533), and is administered by State's Diplomatic Security Service. Rewards over $250,000 must be approved by the Secretary of State. The program can pay to relocate informants and immediate family who fear for their safety. The 1994 "crime bill" (P.L. 103-322) helps relocate aliens and immediate family members in the U.S. who are reward recipients. Expanded participation by the private sector in funding and publicizing such reward programs has been suggested by some observers.

Extradition/Law Enforcement Cooperation. International cooperation in such areas as law enforcement, customs control, and intelligence activities is an important tool in combating international terrorism. One critical law enforcement tool in combating international terrorism is extradition of terrorists. International extradition traditionally has been subject to several limitations, including the refusal to extradite for political or extraterritorial offenses and the refusal of some countries to extradite their nationals. The United States has been encouraging the negotiation of treaties with fewer limitations, in part as a means of facilitating the transfer of wanted terrorists. Because much terrorism involves politically motivated violence, the Department of State has recently sought to curtail the availability of the political offense exception, found in many extradition treaties, to avoid extradition.

Military Force. Although not without difficulties, military force, particularly when wielded by a superpower such as the United States, can carry substantial clout. Proponents of selective use of military force usually emphasize the military's unique skills and specialized equipment. The April 1986 decision to bomb Libya for its alleged role in the bombing of a German discotheque exemplifies use of military force. Other examples are: (1) the 1993 bombing of Iraq's military intelligence headquarters by U.S. forces in response to Iraqi efforts to assassinate former president George Bush during a visit to Kuwait and (2) the August 1998 missile attacks against bases in Afghanistan and a chemical production facility in Sudan.

Concerns about the terrorist threat prompted an extensive buildup of the military's counter-terrorist organization. A special unit known as "Delta Force" at Fort Bragg, NC, has been organized to perform anti-terrorist operations when needed. Details about the unit are secret, but estimates are that it has about 800 assigned personnel.

Use of military force presupposes the ability to identify a terrorist group or sponsor and its location, knowledge often unavailable to law enforcement officials. Risks of military force include (1) military casualties or captives, (2) foreign civilian casualties, (3) retaliation and escalation by terrorist groups, (4) holding the wrong parties responsible, (5) sympathy for the "bullied" victim, and (6) perception that the U.S. ignores rules of international law.

P.L. 104-264 includes a sense of the Senate statement that if evidence suggests "beyond a clear and reasonable doubt" that an act of hostility against any U.S. citizen was a terrorist act sponsored, organized, condoned or directed by any nation, then a state of war should be considered to exist between the United States and that nation.

International Conventions. To date, the United States has joined with the world community in developing all of the major anti-terrorism conventions. These conventions impose on their signatories an obligation either to prosecute offenders or extradite them to permit prosecution for a host of terrorism-related crimes including hijacking vessels and aircraft, taking hostages, and harming diplomats. An important new convention not yet in force is the Convention for the Marking of Plastic Explosives. Implementing legislation is in P.L. 104-132. On December 8, 1999, the U.N. General Assembly adopted the Anti-Terrorism Financing Convention that grew out of G-8 nation endeavors to combat terrorist financing.

Potential Tools

An International Court for Terrorism. Each year bills are introduced urging that an international court be established, perhaps under the U.N., to sit in permanent session to adjudicate cases against persons accused of international terrorist crimes. The court would have broad powers to sentence and punish anyone convicted of such crimes. Critics point out many administrative and procedural problems associated with establishing such a court and making it work, including jurisdictional and enforcement issues. An International Court of Justice in The Hague exists, but it deals with disputes between states and lacks compulsory jurisdiction and enforcement powers.

Media Self-Restraint. For some, the term "media self-restraint" is an oxymoron; the sensational scoop is the Golden Fleece and dull copy is to be avoided. While some of the media struggle to maintain objectivity, they are occasionally manipulated into the role of mediator and often that of publicist of terrorist goals. Though not an international incident, the publication of the Unabomber's "manifesto" illustrated this. Notably, there have been attempts by the media to impose its own rules when covering terrorist incidents. Standards established by the Chicago Sun-Times and Daily News include paraphrasing terrorist demands to avoid unbridled propaganda; banning participation of reporters in negotiations with terrorists; coordinating coverage through supervising editors who are in contact with police authorities; providing thoughtful, restrained, and credible coverage of stories; and allowing only senior supervisory editors to determine what, if any, information should be withheld or deferred. Such standards are far from uniformly accepted. In an intensely competitive profession consisting of a multinational worldwide press corps, someone is likely to break the story.

Policy Reform

On June 5, 2000, the National Commission on Terrorism (NTC), a congressionally mandated bi-partisan body, issued its report which included a blueprint for U.S. counter-terrorism policy with both policy and legislative recommendations.

The NTC report is likely to stimulate strong congressional interest in counter-terrorism policy when the 107th Congress convenes in January 2001. Likely areas of focus are (1) a more proactive counter-terrorism policy; (2) a stronger state sanctions policy; and (3) a more cohesive/better coordinated U.S. federal counter-terrorism policy.

U.S. ORGANIZATION AND PROGRAM RESPONSE

The chain of command on anti-terrorism planning runs from the President through the National Security Council, a representative of which chairs a senior interagency Terrorism Security Group (TSG). The State Department is designated the lead agency for countering terrorism overseas; the Justice Department's Federal Bureau of Investigation (FBI) is the lead agency for domestic terrorism; and the Federal Aviation Administration is the lead for hijackings when a plane's doors are closed. These roles were reaffirmed by Presidential Decision Directive (PDD) no. 39 in June 1995. PDD 62 (Protection Against Unconventional Threats) and PDD 63 (Critical Infrastructure Protection) of May 22, 1998; (1) established with the NSC a National Coordinator for Security, Infrastructure Protection, and Counter-terrorism who also provides "advice" regarding the counter-terrorism budget; (2) established with the NSC two Senior Directors who report to the National Coordinator – one for infrastructure protection and one for counter-terrorism; (3) established a new inter-agency working group primarily focused on domestic preparedness for WMD incidents; and (4) laid out the architecture for critical infrastructure protection. Intelligence information among the various agencies is coordinated by an Intelligence Committee, chaired by a representative of the CIA. An important policy question is whether current organizational structure brings excessive focus on state-sponsored actions at the expense of attention on so-called "gray area" terrorist activity (i.e. terrorist activity not clearly linked to any perpetrator, group, or supporting/sponsoring nation). In light of recent trends in terrorist activity, some suggest an independent comprehensive review of counter-terrorism policy, organizational structure, and preparedness to respond to major terrorist incidents in the United States is warranted. Whether PDD 62, by establishing a national terrorism coordinator at the NSC, takes too much of the terrorism decision-making process out of the realm of congressional oversight is another issue as NSC members generally do not testify before Congress.

A number of Administration programs focus specifically on combating international terrorism. They include the Department of State's (1) Anti-Terrorism Assistance Program (ATA), (2) Counter-Terrorism Research and Development Program, and (3) Diplomatic Security Program. The DOD Authorization Act (Title XIV) for FY1997 (P.L. 104-201) seeks to ensure DOD assistance to federal, state, and local officials in responding to biological, chemical and nuclear emergencies.

On January 22, 1999, President Clinton announced a $10 billion initiative to address terrorism. Included were $1.4 billion to protect against chemical and biological terrorism and $1.46 billion to protect critical systems from cyber and other attacks.

Anti-Terrorism Assistance Program

The State Department's anti-terrorism assistance program provides training and equipment to foreign countries to help them improve their anti-terrorism capabilities. More than 20,000 individuals from 100 countries have received training since the program's inception in 1983 in such skills as crisis management, VIP protection, airport security management, and bomb detection and deactivation. The Administration's FY1998 $18 million request for this program was fully funded at $19 million; the FY1999 request totaled $21 million and was funded at $41 million (which included $20 million from a FY1999 emergency security supplemental appropriations), and the FY2000 request was $23 million.

Counter-Terrorism Research and Development Program

The State Department's Counter-Terrorism Research and Development Program, which is jointly funded by the Departments of State and Defense, constitutes a response to combat the threat posed by increasingly sophisticated equipment and explosives available to terrorist groups. Recent projects include detectors for nuclear materials, decontaminants for chemical and biological weapons, law enforcement and intelligence database software and surveillance technology. The State Department's FY1997-FY2000 budget requests for these programs totaled $1.8 million. DoD's FY2000 request totaled $52.2 with a $54.8 million request projected for FY2001.

Diplomatic Security Program

The Diplomatic Security Program of the State Department is designed to protect U.S. personnel, information and facilities abroad. Providing security guards and counterintelligence awareness are important elements of the program. Detection and investigation of passport and visa fraud is another component of the program.

The Administration's FY2000 request for the Diplomatic Security Program is $226.514 million. One component of the broader program provides protection of international organizations, foreign missions and officials under the Foreign Missions Act of 1982. Security enhancement for U.S. embassies is funded through the "Acquisition and Maintenance of Buildings Abroad" account. The FY1999 request was $640.8 million with $1,030.6 million appropriated.

The State Department's FY2000 request to Congress includes $568 million for embassy security. The Administration included in its State Department request an advance appropriation of $3 billion for FY2001-FY2005. Beginning with a FY2001 baseline of $300 million, the Administration will allocate these funds in additional $150 million increments each year ending with $900 million for FY2005.

Options for Program Enhancement

Numerous options have been proposed to improve the effectiveness of programs designed to combat terrorism. Some notable areas cited for improvement include contingency planning; explosive detection; joint or multinational research, operational and training programs/exercises; nuclear materials safeguarding; and disaster consequence management. Some have suggested that U.S. public diplomacy/media programs could be broadened to support anti-terrorism policy objectives. Cyber security remains an important area for program enhancement. On January 9, 2000, the Administration released a comprehensive plan to combat cyber-terrorism including $2 billion in proposed spending next year to make the nation's computer systems less vulnerable to attack. Plan elements include: (1) enhanced funding for research and development; (2) creation of an ROTC-type corps of information specialists; and (3) creation of a national institute charged with forging a research partnership with the private sector.

STATE-SUPPORTED TERRORISM

The Secretary of State maintains a list of countries that have "repeatedly provided support for acts of international terrorism." Data supporting this list is drawn from the intelligence community. Listed countries are subject to severe U.S. export controls, particularly of dual use technology, and selling them military equipment is prohibited. Section 6(j) of the 1979 Export Administration Act stipulates that a validated license shall be required for export of controlled items and technology to any country on the list, and that the Secretaries of Commerce and State must notify the House Committee on Foreign Affairs, and both the Senate Committees on Banking, Housing, and Urban Affairs, and Foreign Relations, at least 30 days before issuing any validated license required by this Act. In addition, Section 509(a) of the 1986 omnibus anti-terrorism act (P.L. 99-399) bars export of munitions list items to countries on the terrorism list. Indirect state sponsorship or sponsorship by proxy is addressed in a second State Department terrorist list (required by P.L. 104-132) – which is distinct from the list of state sponsors generally referred to as the "list" – prohibits the sale of arms to nations not fully cooperating with U.S. anti-terrorism efforts. Strong language critical of Greece in *Patterns 1999* prompts some to question whether Greece should be included in the latter category of nations. The current list of countries not fully cooperating includes seven state supporters plus Afghanistan. P.L. 104-132 also requires the withholding of foreign assistance to nations providing lethal military aid to countries on the list of state sponsors.

Adding and Removing Countries on the List

In late January each year, under the provisions of Section 6(j) of the Export Administration Act of 1979, as amended, the Secretary of Commerce in consultation with the Secretary of State provides congress with a list of countries supporting terrorism. Compilation of the list is the result of an ongoing process. Throughout the year the Department of State gathers data on terrorist activity worldwide, and then beginning about November, the list is formally reviewed. Each new determination under Section 6(j) of the Act must also be published in the Federal Register.

Paragraph 6(j)(4) of the Export Administration Act prohibits removing a country from the list unless the President first submits a report to the House Committee on Foreign Affairs, and the Senate Committees on Banking, Housing, and Urban Affairs, and Foreign Relations. When a government comes to power (i.e., a government different from that in power at the time of the last determination), the President's report, submitted before the proposed rescission would take effect, must certify that (1) there has been a fundamental change in the leadership and policies of the government of the country concerned (this means an actual change of government as a result of an election, coup, or some other means); (2) the new government is not supporting acts of international terrorism; and (3) the new government has provided assurances that it will not support acts of international terrorism in the future. When the same government is in power, the President's report – **submitted at least 45 days before the proposed rescission would take effect** – must justify the rescission and certify that; (1) the government concerned has not provided support for international terrorism during the preceding 6-month period; and (2) the government concerned has provided assurances that it will not support acts of international terrorism in the future. Congress can let the President's action take effect, or pass legislation to block it, the latter most likely over the President's veto. To date Congress has passed no such legislation or resolution, although Syria would be the likely target of such endeavors, should the Administration prematurely seek its removal from the terrorism list. Patterns 1999 notes that "if a state sponsor meets the criteria from being dropped from the terrorism list, it will be removed – notwithstanding other differences we may have with a country's other policies and actions."

Countries on the List

Currently seven countries are on the "terrorism list": Cuba, Iran, Iraq, Libya, North Korea, Sudan and Syria. (For further information on states sponsoring international terrorism, see *Patterns of Global Terrorism (Patterns 1999)*, Department of State, April 2000). Of the seven, five are Middle Eastern nations with predominantly Muslim populations. Of these, Iran, Iraq, could currently be characterized on one extreme as active supporters of terrorism: nations that use terrorism as an instrument of policy or warfare beyond their borders. Iran, Iraq, and Libya are major oil producers, holding 17% of the world's remaining oil and producing, in 1994, 5.5% of the world's oil supply, 31% of Europe's (OECD) oil consumption, and 9% of Japan's. Such dependence on oil complicates universal support for sanctions against these nations.

On the other extreme one might place countries such as Cuba or North Korea, which at the height of the Cold War were more active, but in recent years have seemed to settle for a more passive role of granting ongoing safe haven to previously admitted individual terrorists. Closer to the middle of an active/passive spectrum is Libya, which grants safe haven to wanted terrorists. Syria, though not formally detected in an active role since 1986, reportedly uses groups in Syria and Lebanon to project power into Israel and allows groups to train in territory under its control, placing it somewhere in the middle to active end of the spectrum. And Sudan, which allows sites for training, remains an enigma. Although Sudan has been considered primarily a passive supporter, charges have been made that Sudan was actively involved in a 1995 attempt to assassinate Egyptian President Hosni Mubarak.

A complex challenge facing those charged with compiling and maintaining the list is the degree to which diminution of hard evidence of a government's active involvement indicates a real change in behavior, particularly when a past history of active support or use of terrorism as an instrument of foreign policy has been well established. Removing a country from the list is likely to result in some level of confrontation with Congress, so the bureaucratically easier solution is to maintain the status quo, or add to the list, but not to delete from it.

Iran. In a change from *Patterns 1998, Patterns 1999* names Iran as the most active state sponsor of terrorism despite acknowledged political changes in Iran during 1999. Iran continues to be deeply involved in the planning and execution of terrorist acts by its own agents and surrogate groups. It provides ongoing direction, safe haven, funding, training, weapons and other support to a variety of radical Islamic terrorist groups including Hizballah in Lebanon, as well as Hammas and Palestinian Islamic Jihad (PIJ) to undermine the Middle East peace process. There are press reports that Iran is building a terrorist infrastructure in the region by providing political indoctrination, military training, and financial help to dissident Shia groups in neighboring countries, including Kuwait, Bahrain, and Saudi Arabia. Iran has reportedly concentrated efforts to make Sudan a center for terrorist training and activities and reportedly continues to conduct assassinations of writers and political dissidents beyond its borders. Iran was placed on the terrorism list in January 1984. President Clinton has halted U.S. trade with Iran and barred U.S. companies from any involvement in the Iranian oil sector. The threat perceived from Iran as a leading supporter of terrorism is substantially raised by reports that Iran is acquiring nuclear technology and seeking nuclear weapons technology.

Iraq. On September 13, 1990, Iraq was placed once again on the terrorism list, after having been removed in 1982. Iraq's ability to instigate terror has been curbed by U.S. and U.N. sanctions which were imposed after the Kuwait invasion. Nevertheless, *Patterns 1999* indicates that Saddam Hussein's regime continues to murder dissidents and provide a safe haven for a variety of Palestinian rejectionist groups. There are numerous claims that the Iraqi intelligence is behind killings and at least one planned bombing during 1999. Iraq also provides active assistance to the MEK, a terrorist group opposed to the Teheran regime. In the past, Iraq has temporarily expelled terrorists, only to invite them back later.

Libya. Libya has a long history of involvement in international terrorism. Libya was placed on the terrorism list when it was started in December 1979 and approximately $1 billion in bank deposits belonging to Libya are frozen by the United States. Libyan terrorism has been sharply reduced after imposition of U.N. sanctions in the wake of Libyan involvement in the bombings of Pan Am flight 103 and in the 1989 bombing of French UTA flight 772 that killed 170 persons, including seven Americans. Evidence suggests Libya has not abandoned its support for international terrorism as an instrument of foreign policy, and it still refuses to hand over some accused of terrorist acts. Through 1998, Libya continued to support groups opposed to the Mid-East peace process that engage in violence. Nevertheless, the response of the international community and U.S. Congress (P.L. 104-172) seems to have been relatively effective in restraining the level of Libya's outlaw behavior and may provide one model for future international action. There is no evidence of Libyan involvement in recent acts of international terrorism. In April 2000, Libya took what *Patterns 1999* notes as "an important step by surrendering...two Libyans accused of bombing Pan Am flight 103...in 1988."

Syria. Syria was placed on the first terrorism list in December 1979. It is generally believed within the western community that Syria has a long history of using terrorists to advance its own interests. The United States has said that it has no evidence of Syrian government direct involvement in terrorism since 1986. Informed sources suggest, however, that the Syrian government remains active, hiding behind the sophisticated operational level of their intelligence services and their ability to mask such involvement. Many major terrorist groups are known to maintain an active presence (including training camps and operational headquarters) in Syria or in Syrian-controlled Lebanon and Syria has allowed Iran to supply Hizballah with weaponry via Damascus. Providing such support, free movement, and safe haven has caused prominent Members of Congress to contend that Syria should remain on the terrorism list, and Administration spokespersons have firmly maintained in testimony before Congress that until this problem is resolved, Syria will remain on the list. In contrast, the Administration has made it clear to Syria that it will consider removing Syria from the list should a peace treaty with Israel be signed. Some observers argue that Syria should continue to be subject to U.S. sanctions because of involvement in drug trafficking by some of its ruling elites and their alleged involvement in counterfeiting of U.S. currency.

Sudan. Sudan was added to the terrorism list in August 1993. Sudan continues to harbor members of some of the world's most violent organizations and according to *Patterns 1999* continues to serve as a refuge, nexus, and training hub for a number of terrorist organizations including Hizballah, Hamas, and bin Laden's al-Qaida organization. Egypt and Ethiopia have charged the Sudanese government with involvement in a failed assassination attempt against President Hosni Mubarak while in Ethiopia in June 1995. On September 11, 1995, the Organization for

African Unity (OAU), in an unprecedented action criticizing a member, passed a resolution calling on Sudan to extradite three suspects charged in the assassination attempt to Ethiopia. The U.N. Security Council has also demanded extradition of the three suspects. Sudan continues to permit its territory to be used by Iran to transport weapons to Islamic extremist groups and as a meeting place for Iranian-backed terrorist groups.

Cuba. Fidel Castro's government has a long history of providing arms and training to terrorist organizations. A cold war carryover, Cuba was added to the 1982 U.S. list of countries supporting international terrorism based on its support for the M-19 guerrilla organization in Columbia. *Patterns 1999* does not cite evidence that Cuban officials were directly involved in sponsoring an act of terrorism in 1999, but notes that Havana remains a safe haven to several international terrorists. The report noted that Cuba no longer actively supports armed struggles in Latin America or elsewhere. Nevertheless, Havana continues to maintain close ties to other state sponsors of terrorism. The Castro regime also reportedly maintains close ties with leftist insurgent groups in Latin America.

North Korea. North Korea was added to the "official" list of countries supporting terrorism because of its implication in the bombing of a South Korean airliner on November 29, 1987, which killed 115 persons. According to the State Department, North Korea is not conclusively linked to any terrorist acts since 1987. A North Korean spokesman in 1993 condemned all forms of terrorism, and said his country resolutely opposed the encouragement and support of terrorism. A similar statement was made in November 1995. Nevertheless, North Korea continues to provide political sanctuary to members of a group that hijacked a Japan Airlines flight in 1970 and may be linked to the murder of a South Korean diplomat in Vladivostoc in 1996. *Patterns 1999* notes that North Korea has made "some positive statements condemning terrorism in all its forms" and has stressed that actions triggering removal from the list "are consistent with its stated policies."

An Informal Watchlist?

Some suggest that there is a utility in drawing to Congress' attention countries that do not currently qualify for inclusion in the terrorism list but where added scrutiny may be warranted. Such a list would be similar to the Attorney General's National Security Threat List that includes sponsors or international terrorism, the activities of which warrant monitoring by the FBI within the United States. Although informal, it would be controversial and speculative. But it would reflect legitimate concerns of those in the intelligence and policy community and might serve as an informal warning mechanism to countries that their activities are being scrutinized. For example, the State Department warned Pakistan in January 1993 that it was under "active continuing review" to determine whether it should be place on the terrorism list. When the list came out in April 1993, Pakistan was not on it. Sudan was also warned that it was being subjected to special review prior to its being placed on the terrorism list in August 1993.

Currently, some informally discussed candidates for such a list include (1) **Afghanistan,** which *Patterns 1999* characterizes as "the primary safe haven for terrorists" – concerns are that Islamic fundamentalist terrorists linked to numerous international plots continue to train and operate out of the country and/or enter or exit with impunity, and more specifically that the Taliban continues to offer sanctuary to Osama bin Laden and his associated terror networks; (2) **Pakistan** – *Patterns 1999* notes that Pakistan has tolerated terrorists living and moving freely within its territory; supported groups that engage in violence in Kashmir; and provided indirect support for terrorists in Afghanistan; (3) **Yugoslavia** – concerns remain over potential use of terrorism in reaction to NATO military operations. Another concern is that militant Iranian elements remaining in the territory of former Yugoslavia may resort to terrorist violence against European nations and the United States; (4) **Lebanon** – growing concern exists over terrorists groups operating with impunity from there, often under Syrian protection; (5) **Greece** – which *Patterns 1999* describes as "one of the weakest links in Europe's efforts against terrorism" and where the absence of strong government measures allows terrorists "to act with virtual impunity;" and (6) **Yemen** – a growing safe haven for international terrorist groups where a growing kidnapping industry flourishes. *Patterns 1999* also reflects a growing concern in policy circles that **Chechnya** may increasingly become a magnet and rallying center for Islamic radicals and notes that concern exists that "increased radicalization of Islamist populations connected to the **Chechnya** conflict would encourage violence and spread instability elsewhere in Russia and beyond."

CRITICAL INFRASTRUCTURES: BACKGROUND AND EARLY IMPLEMENTATION OF PDD-63

John D. Moteff

LATEST DEVELOPMENTS

The Information Technology sector announced the formation of its Information Sharing and Analysis Center (ISAC). ISAC members include major hardware, software, and e-commerce firms including AT&T, IBM, Cisco, Intel, Microsoft, and Oracle. For information in ISACs, see page 10.

Before leaving office, President Clinton announced his selection of nominees to serve on the National Infrastructure Assurance Council.

The Bush Administration, as part of its overall review of White House offices and responsibilities is reviewing its options for overseeing and coordinating protection of the nation's critical infrastructures. Based on media reports, the Bush Administration has received a number of recommendations to modify the organizational structures established by the Clinton Administration.

INTRODUCTION

Certain socio-economic activities are vital to the day-to-day functioning and security of the country; for example, transportation of goods and people, communications, banking and finance, and the supply and distribution of electricity and water. These activities and services have been referred to as components of the nation's critical infrastructure. Domestic security and our ability to monitor, deter, and respond to outside hostile acts also depend on some of these activities as well as other more specialized activities like intelligence gathering and command and control of police and military forces. A serious disruption of these activities and capabilities could have a major impact on the country's well being.[1]

These activities and capabilities are supported by an array of physical assets, processes, information, and organizations forming what is being called the nation's critical infrastructures. The country's critical infrastructures are growing increasingly complex, relying on computers and, now, computer networks to operate efficiently and reliably. The growing complexity and the interconnectedness resulting from networking means that a disruption in one may lead to disruptions in others.

Disruptions can be caused by any number of factors: poor design, operator error, physical destruction due to natural causes, (earthquakes, lightening strikes, etc.) or physical destruction due to intentional human actions (theft, arson, sabotage, etc.). Over the years, operators of these infrastructures have taken measures to guard against and to quickly respond to many of these risks. However, the growing dependency of these systems on information technologies and computer networks introduces a new vector by which problems can be introduced.[2]

Of particular concern is the threat posed by "hackers" who can gain unauthorized access to a system and who could destroy, corrupt, steal, or monitor information vital to the operation of the system. Unlike arsonists or saboteurs, hackers can gain access from remote locations. The ability to detect and deter their actions is still being developed. While infrastructure operators are also taking measures to guard against and respond to cyber attacks, there is concern that the number of "on-line" operations is growing faster than security awareness and the use of sound security measures.

Hackers range from mischievous teenagers, to criminals, to spies, to foreign military organizations. While the more commonly reported incidents involve mischievous teenagers (or adults) or self-proclaimed "electronic anarchists", the primary concern is that criminals, spies, and military

---

[1] As a reminder of how dependent society is on its infrastructure, in May 1998, PanAmSat's Galaxy IV satellite's on-board controller malfunctioned, disrupting service to an estimated 80-90% of the nation's pagers, causing problems for hospitals trying to reach doctors on call, emergency workers, and people trying to use their credit cards at gas pumps, to name but a few.

[2] Efforts to merge the computer systems of Norfolk Southern and Conrail after their merger in June 1999 caused a series of mishaps leaving trains misrouted, crews mis-scheduled, and products lost. As of January 2000, problems still persisted. See, "Merged Railroads Still Plagued by IT Snafus," *Computerworld*, January 17, 2000, pp. 20-21.

personnel from around the world who appear to be perfecting their hacking skills and who may pose a potential strategic threat to the reliable operations of our critical infrastructures.[3]

THE PRESIDENT'S COMMISSION ON CRITICAL INFRASTRUCTURE PROTECTION

In the FY1996 Department of Defense Authorization bill (P.L. 104-106) Congress required the President to report to Congress a national policy on protecting the nation's information infrastructure from strategic attack. Partially in response to that legislation and also to internal discussions on national security, President Clinton established the President's Commission on Critical Infrastructure Protection (PCCIP) in July 1996. Its tasks were to: report to the President the scope and nature of the vulnerabilities and threats to the nation's critical infrastructures (focusing primarily on cyber threats); recommend a comprehensive national policy and implementation plan for protecting critical infrastructures; determine legal and policy issues raised by proposals to increase protections; and propose statutory and regulatory changes necessary to effect recommendations.

The PCCIP released its report to President Clinton in October 1997.[4] While the Commission found no immediate crisis threatening the nation's infrastructures, it did find reason to take action. The rapid growth of a computer-literate population (implying a greater pool of potential hackers), the inherent vulnerabilities of common protocols in computer networks, the easy availability of hacker "tools" (available on many websites), and the fact that the basic tools of the hacker (computer, modem, telephone line) are the same essential technologies used by the general population indicated to the Commission that the threat and vulnerability exist.

---

[3] The Director of the Central Intelligence Agency testified before the Senate Committee on Governmental Affairs (June 24, 1998) that a number of countries are incorporating information warfare into their military doctrine and training and developing operational capability. It should be noted that the U.S. military is probably the leader in developing both offensive and defensive computer warfare techniques and doctrine.

[4] President's Commission on Critical Infrastructure Protection, *Critical Foundations: Protecting America's Infrastructures*, October 1997.

The Commission's general recommendation was that greater cooperation and communication between the private sector and government was needed. Much of the nation's critical infrastructure is owned and operated by the private sector. As seen by the Commission, the government's primary role (aside from protecting its own infrastructures) is to collect and disseminate the latest information on intrusion techniques, threat analysis, and ways to defend against hackers.

The Commission also proposed a strategy for action:

- Facilitate greater cooperation and communication between the private sector and appropriate government agencies by: setting a top level policy-making office in the White House; establishing a council that includes corporate executives, state and local government officials, and cabinet secretaries; and setting up information clearinghouses;
- Develop a real-time capability of attack warning;
- Establish and promote a comprehensive awareness and education program;
- Streamline and clarify elements of the legal structure to support assurance measures (including clearing jurisdictional barriers to pursuing hackers electronically); and,
- Expand research and development in technologies and techniques, especially technologies that allow for greater detection of intrusions.

The Commission's report underwent interagency review to determine how to respond. That review led to a Presidential Decision Directive released in May 1998.

PRESIDENTIAL DECISION DIRECTIVE NO. 63

Presidential Decision Directive No. 63 (PDD-63)[5] set as a national goal the ability to protect the nation's critical infrastructure from intentional attacks (both physical and cyber) by the year 2003. According to the PDD,

---

[5] See, The *Clinton's Administration's Policy on Critical Infrastructure Protection: Presidential Decision Directive 63*, White Paper, May 22, 1998, which can be found on [http://www.ciao.ncr.gov/ciao_document_library/paper598.html].

any interruptions in the ability of these infrastructures to provide their goods and services must by "brief, infrequent, manageable, geographically isolated, and minimally detrimental to the welfare of the United States."[6]

PDD-63 identified the following activities whose critical infrastructures should be protected: information and communications; banking and finance; water supply; aviation, highways, mass transit, pipelines, rail, and waterborne commerce; emergency and law enforcement services; emergency, fire, and continuity of government services; public health services; electric power, oil and gas production, and storage. In addition, the PDD identified four activities where the federal government controls the critical infrastructure: internal security and federal law enforcement; foreign intelligence; foreign affairs; and national defense.

A lead agency was assigned to each of these "sectors" (see **Table 1**). Each lead agency was to appoint a **Sector Liaison Official** to interact with appropriate private sector organizations. The private sector was encouraged to select a **Sector Coordinator** to work with the agency's sector liaison official. Together, the liaison official, sector coordinator, and all affected parties will contribute to a sectoral security plan which will be integrated into a **National Infrastructure Assurance Plan** (see **Table 1**). Each of the activities performed primarily by the federal government also are assigned to lead agency who will appoint a **Functional Coordinator** to coordinate efforts similar to those made by the Sector Liaisons.

The PDD created the position of National Coordinator for Security, Infrastructure Protection, and Counter-terrorism, who reports to the President through the Assistant to the President for National Security Affairs.[7] Among his many duties the National Coordinator chairs the **Critical Infrastructure Coordination Group**. This Group is the primary interagency working group for developing and implementing policy and for coordinating the federal government's own internal security measures. The Group includes high level representatives from the lead agencies (including the Sector Liaisons), the National Economic Council, and all other relevant agencies.

---

[6] Ibid.

[7] President Clinton designated Richard Clarke, Special Assistant to the President for Global Affairs, National Security Council, as National Coordinator.

Table 1. Lead Agencies

Department/Agency	Sector/Function
Commerce	Information and Communication
Treasury	Banking
EPA	Water
Transportation	Transportation
Justice	Emergency Law Enforcement
Federal Emergency Management Agency	Emergency Fire Service
Health and Human Services	Emergency Medicine
Energy	Electric Power, Gas, and Oil
Justice	Law Enforcement and International Security
Director of Central Intelligence	Intelligence
State	Foreign Affairs
Defense	National Defense

Each federal agency is responsible for securing its own critical infrastructure and shall designate a Critical Infrastructure Assurance Officer (CIAO) to assume that responsibility. The agency's current Chief Information Officer (CIO) may double in that capacity. In those cases where the CIO and the CIAO are different, the CIO is responsible for assuring the agency's information assets (databases, software, computers), while the CIAO is responsible for any other assets that make up that agency's critical infrastructure. The lead agencies listed in the Directive and others listed as primary agencies (Federal Bureau of Investigations, Central Intelligence Agency, Veterans Affairs, and the National Security Agency) were given 180 days from the signing of the Directive to develop their plans. Those plans are to be fully implemented within 2 years and updated every 2 years.

The PDD set up a **National Infrastructure Assurance Council**. The Council will be a panel that includes private operators of infrastructure assets and officials from state and local government officials and relevant federal agencies. The Council will meet periodically and provide reports to the President as appropriate. The National Coordinator will act as the Executive Director of the Council

The PDD also called for a **National Infrastructure Assurance Plan.** The plan is to integrate the plans from each of the sectors mentioned above and should consider the following: a vulnerability assessment, including the minimum essential capability required of the sector's infrastructure to meet its purpose; remedial plans to reduce the sector's vulnerability; warning requirements and procedures; response strategies; reconstitution of services; education and awareness programs; research and development needs; intelligence strategies; needs and opportunities for international cooperation; and legislative and budgetary requirements.

The PDD also set up a National Plan Coordination Staff to support the plan's development. This function is performed by the **Critical Infrastructure Assurance Office** (CIAO, not to be confused with the agencies' Critical Infrastructure Assurance Officers) and was placed in the Department of Commerce. CIAO supports the National Coordinator's efforts to integrate the sectoral plans into a National Plan, supports individual agencies in developing their internal plans, helps coordinate a national education and awareness programs, and provides legislative and public affairs support.

In addition to the above activities, the PDD called for studies on specific topics. These include issues of: liability that might arise from private firms participating in an information sharing process; legal impediments to information sharing; classification of information and granting of clearances (efforts to share threat and vulnerability information with private sector CEOs has been hampered by the need to convey that information in a classified manner); information sharing with foreign entities; and the merits of mandating, subsidizing or otherwise assisting in the provision of insurance for selected infrastructure providers.

Most of the Directive established policy-making and oversight bodies making use of existing agency authorities and expertise. However, the PDD also addressed operational concerns. The Directive called for a national capability to detect and respond to attacks while they are in progress. Although not specifically identified in the Directive, the Clinton Administration has proposed establishing a **Federal Instruction Detection Network (FIDNET)**, that would, together with the **Federal Computer Intrusion Response Capability (FedCIRC)** effort begun just prior to PDD-63, meet this goal. Current proposals have the General Services Administration managing both efforts, but both would be staffed by experts from across the government. FIDNET would help agencies detect intrusions and FedCIRC would help them respond. The Directive did explicitly give the Federal Bureau of Investigation the authority to expand its existing computer crime capabilities into a **National Infrastructure Protection Center (NIPC)**. According to the Directive, the NIPC is to be the focal point for federal threat assessment, vulnerability analysis, early warning capability, law enforcement investigations, and response coordination. All agencies are required to forward to the NIPC information about threats and actual attacks on their infrastructure as well as attacks made on private sector infrastructures of which they become aware. Presumably, FIDNET and FedCIRC would feed into the NIPC. According to the Directive, the NIPC would be linked electronically to the rest of the federal government and use warning and response expertise located throughout the federal government. According to the Directive, the NIPC will also be the conduit for information sharing with the private sector through equivalent **Information Sharing and Analysis Center(s)** operated by the private sector.

While the FBI was given the lead, the NIPC also includes the Department of Defense, the Intelligence Community, and a representative from all lead agencies. Depending on the level of threat or the character of the intrusion, the NIPC may be placed in direct support of either the Department of Defense or the Intelligence Community.

IMPLEMENTING PDD-63: STATUS AS FEBRUARY 2001

Selection of Sector Liaison Officials and Functional Coordinators.

All lead agencies and lead functional agencies have appointed their Sector Liaison Officials and Functional Coordinators.

Identifying and Selecting Sector Coordinators. The identification of sector coordinators is proceeding with mixed results. The table below shows those individuals or groups that have agreed to act as Coordinators or have been approached by the lead agency.

Different sectors present different challenges to identifying a coordinator. Some sectors are more diverse than others (e.g. transportation includes rail, air, waterways, and highways; information and communications include computers, software, wire and wireless communications) and raises the issue of how to have all the relevant players represented. Other sectors are fragmented consisting of small or local entities. Some sectors, such as banking, telecommunications, and energy have more experience than others in working with the federal government and/or working collectively to assure the performance of their systems.

Besides such structural issues are ones related to competition. Inherent in the exercise is asking competitors to cooperate. In some cases it is asking competing industries to cooperate. This cooperation not only raises issues of trust among firms, but also concerns regarding anti-trust rules. Also, having these groups in direct communication with the federal government raises questions about their relationship to the federal government as governed by the Federal advisory Committee Act (5 USC Appendix) and how the Freedom of Information Act (5 USC 552) applies to them and the information that may be exchanged.

For the most part, the sector coordinators selected to date have undertaken awareness and education activities not only to acquaint their constituents with the threats and risks of cyber attack on their systems (which in many cases is already known) but also about the efforts and goals of PDD-63. Typically these activities have been carried out through regular trade/professional association committee meetings, conferences, etc.

Table 2. Sector Coordinators

Lead Agency	Identified Sector Coordinators
Commerce	A consortium of 3 associations: Information Technology Assn. Of America; Telecommunications Industry Assn.; U.S. Telephone Assn.
Treasury	Steven Katz – Citigroup
EPA	Assn. Of Metropolitan Water Agencies
Energy	North American Electric Reliability Council and National Petroleum Council
Transportation	Association of American Railroads (under discussion)
Health and Human Services	
FEMA	
Justice	

Of the largely privately operated sectors, only the transportation sector has yet to identify a Coordinator. The Department of Transportation has contacted the Association of American Railroads to discuss their interest in acting as Coordinator for the railroad industry after talks with the National Defense Transportation Association (which include rail and air) decided it was too small. FEMA, too, is still trying to identify a group that could represent the country's emergency/fire service providers. FEMA has discussed cyber issues with state and local governments in the context of the Y2K problem, but has not identified a central coordinator for handling cyber attacks on state – or local – operated infrastructures.[8] Nor has the Department of Health and Human Services identified a central coordinator for the emergency medical community. The Department of Justice also has not identified a single coordinator for emergency law enforcement but is using existing outreach programs at the FBI and the NIPC to promote awareness and education activities.

Appointment of the National Infrastructure Assurance Council. The Administration released and Executive Order (13130) in July 1999, formally establishing the council. Just prior to leaving office, President Clinton put forward the names of 18 people for nomination.[9]

Selection of Agency CIAOs. All agencies have made permanent or acting CIAO appointments.

Internal Agency Plans. All of the lead and primary agencies designated in PDD-63 met the initial deadline for submitting their internal plans for protecting their own critical infrastructures from attacks and for responding to intrusions. The Critical Infrastructure Assurance Office assembled an expert team to review the plans. The plans were assessed in 12 areas including schedule/milestone planning, resource requirements, and knowledge of existing authorities and guidance. The assessment team handed back the initial plans with comments. Agencies were given 90 days to respond to these comments.

A second tier of agencies identified by the National Coordinator were also required to submit plans. These were Agriculture, Education, Housing and Urban Development, Labor, Interior, General Services Administration,

---

[8] The New Mexico Critical Infrastructure Assurance Council, an offshoot of the FBI's InfraGard efforts in the state, includes the state government and other state and local agencies. The Council is referenced in the *Nation Plan for Information Systems Protection*. See, **National Critical Infrastructure Plan**, below.

[9] White House Press Release dated January 18, 2000.

National Aeronautics and Space Administration and the Nuclear Regulatory Commission. Their plans were turned in by the end of February 1999. These, too, were reviewed by the tam and sent back with comments. Of the 22 agencies required to submit plans, 16 resubmitted plans in response to first round comments.

Initially the process of reviewing these agency plans was to continue until all concerns were addressed. Over the summer of 1999, however, review efforts slowed and subsequent reviews were put on hold as the efficacy of the reviews was debated. Some within the CIAO felt that the plans were too general and lacked a clear understanding of what constituted a "critical asset" and the interdependencies of those assets. As a result of that internal debate, the CIAO has redirected its resources to institute a new program called Project Matrix. Project Matrix is a three-step process by which an agency can identify and assess its most critical assets, identify the dependencies of those assets on other systems, including those beyond the direct control of the agency, and prioritize. CIAO has offered this analysis to 14 agencies, some not bound to PDD-63 (e.g. Social Security Administration and the Securities and Exchange Commission). Participation by the agencies is voluntary. Responsibility for review of agency critical infrastructure plans has been given to the National Institute of Standards and technology, the support for which appeared in the Clinton Administration's FY2001 budget request (see Appendix).

According to the National Plan released in January 2000 (see Table 3), all primary and secondary agencies are to have completed preliminary vulnerability analyses and to have outlined proposed remedial actions. Again, according to the National Plan, those remedial actions were to be budgeted for and submitted as part of the agencies' FY2001 budgets submissions to the Office of Management and Budget and every year thereafter. However, given the discussion above, the comprehensiveness of these plans at this time may be in question.

National Critical Infrastructure Plan. The Administration, after some delay, released Version 1.0 of its National Plan for Information Systems Protection in January 2000. The plan focuses primarily on efforts within the federal government, and dividing those between government-wide efforts and those unique to the national security community. A second component dealing with the private sector and state and local governments is in a formative stage. There is also to be developed a plan for the physical protection of critical assets. The Plan (159 pages) will not be summarized here in any detail.   The reader is referred to the CIAO website ([http://www.ciao.gov]) for either the executive summary or the full text of the Plan.   Essentially, the Plan identifies 10 "programs" under three broad objectives (see Table 3).

Each program contains some specific actions to be taken, capabilities to be established, and dates by which these shall be accomplished.   Other activities, capabilities, and dates are more general (e.g. during FY2001).

The Plan includes a number of new initiatives identified by the Clinton Administration.   These are identified in the appendix of this report.   Of course, the ability to meet some of these milestones will depend on the willingness of Congress to appropriate funds to carry them out.

Table 3. National Plan for Information Systems Protection Version 1.0

Goal: Achieve a critical information systems defense with an initial operating capability by December 2000, and a full operating capability by May 2003…that ensures any interruption or manipulation of these critical functions must be brief, infrequent, manageable, geographically isolated, and minimally detrimental to the welfare of the United States.	
Objectives	Programs
Prepare and Prevent	ID critical infrastructures and interdependencies and address vulnerabilities
Detect and Respond	Detect attacks and unauthorized intrusions
	Develop robust intelligence and law enforcement capabilities consistent with the law
	Share attack warning and information in a timely manner
	Create capabilities for response, reconstitution, and recovery
Build Strong Foundations	
	Train and employ adequate numbers of information security specialists
	Make Americans aware of the need for improved cyber-security
	Adopt legislation and appropriations in support of effort
	At every step of the process ensure full protection of American citizens' civil liberties, rights to privacy, and rights to protection of proprietary information

Information Sharing and Analysis Center (ISAC). PDD-63 envisaged an ISAC to be the private sector counterpart of the FBI's National Infrastructure Protection Center (NIPC), collecting and sharing incident and response information among its members and facilitating information exchange between government and the private sector. It is one of the critical recommendations made in the PCCIP and probably one of the hardest to realize. While the Directive conceived of a single center serving the entire private sector, the idea now is that each sector would have its own center. The Clinton Administration's FY2000 budget request included $8 million, $1 million for each of the primary liaison agencies, to support the establishment of ISACs for each sector. Progress in forming sector ISACs has been mixed.

Twenty-two of the nation's largest banks, securities, firms, insurance companies and investment companies have joined together in a limited liability corporation to form a banking and finance industry ISAC. An executive of Bank America chairs the CEO Council that acts as the corporation's board. The group has contracted with an Internet service provider[10] (ISP) to design and operate the ISAC. Individual firms feed raw computer network traffic data to the ISAC. The ISP maintains a database and analyzes it for suspicious behavior and provides its customers with summary reports. If suspicious behavior is detected, the analysis may be forwarded to the federal government. Anonymity is maintained between participants and outside the ISAC. The ISP will forward to its customers alerts and other information provided by the federal government. The ISAC became operational in October 1999.

The telecommunications industry has agreed to establish an ISAC through the National Coordinating Center (NCC). The NCC is a government-industry partnership that coordinates responses to disruptions in the National Communications System. Unlike the banking and finance ISAC that uses a third party for centralized monitoring and analysis, each member firm of the NCC will monitor and analyze its own networks. If a firm suspects its network(s) have been breached, it will discuss the incident(s) within the NCC. The NCC members will decide whether the suspected behavior is serious enough to report to the appropriate federal authorities. Anonymity will be maintained outside the NCC. Any

---

[10] The ISP is Global Integrity, a subsidiary of Science Applications International Corp. (SAIC).

communication between federal authorities and member firms will take place through the NCC; this includes incident response and requests for additional information.[11]

The electric power sector, too, has established a decentralized ISAC through its North American Electricity Reliability Council (NAERC). Much like the NCC, NAERC already monitors and coordinates responses to disruptions in the nation's supply of electricity. It is in this forum that information security issues and incidents will be shared. The National Petroleum Council is still considering setting up an ISAC with its members.

In January 2001, the information technology industry announced its plans to form as ISAC. Members include 19 major hardware, software, and e-commerce firms, including AT&T, IBM, Cisco, Microsoft, Intel, and Oracle. The ISAC will be overseen by a board made up of members and operated by Internet Security Systems.

The country's water authorities are not leaning toward any centralized analysis or reporting function. Individual water authorities have existing lines of communications with the FBI through which they could report suspicious behavior. The same could be true for the other local and state emergency services sectors.

In addition to these individual sectors setting up or contemplating ISACs, a number of sectors have formed a **Partnership for Critical Infrastructure Security** to share information and strategies and to identify interdependencies across sectoral lines. The Partnership is a private sector initiative. A preliminary meeting was held in December 1999 and five working groups were established (Interdependencies/Vulnerability Assessment, Cross-Sector Information Sharing, Legislation and Policy, Research and Development, and Organization). The working groups meet every other month. The federal government is not officially part of the Partnership, but the CIAO acts as a liaison and has provided administrative support for meetings. Sector Liaison from lead agencies are considered ex officio members. Some entities not yet part of their own industry group (e.g. some hospitals and pharmaceutical firms) are interested in participating in the Partnership.

Also, besides the efforts of the lead agencies to assist their sectors in considering ISACs, the NIPC offers private sector firms from across all industries a program called INFRAGARD. The program includes an Alert

---

[11] Federal agencies sit on the NCC, including the NSA. One could assume that knowledge of incidents discussed in the NCC could find its way to federal investigatory authorities without formally being reported.

Network. Participants in the program agree to supply the FBI with two reports when they suspect an intrusion of their systems has occurred. One report is "sanitized" of sensitive information and the other provides more detailed description of the intrusion. The FBI will help the participant respond to the intrusion. In addition, all participants are sent periodic updates on what is known about recent intrusion techniques. The NPIC is working to set up local INFRAGARD chapters that can work with each other and regional FBI field offices. In January 2001, the FBI announced it had finished establishing INFRAGARD chapters in each of its 56 field offices.

ISSUES

Administrative. While the Directive deals with infrastructure issues beyond just computer systems and also considers physical protections, the Directive primarily is concerned with "cyber" threats and vulnerabilities and, therefore, is an extension of the government's efforts in computer security. The Directive sought to use existing authorities and expertise as much as possible in assigning responsibilities. Nevertheless, the Directive does set up new entities that, at least at first glance, assume responsibilities previously assigned to others. One question is to what extent does the Directive duplicate, supersede, incorporate, or overturn existing computer security efforts?

For example, the Paperwork Reduction Act of 1995 (P.L. 104-13) placed the responsibility for establishing government-wide information resources management policy with the Director of the Office of Management and Budget. Those policies are outlined in OMB Circular A-130. Appendix III of the Circular incorporates responsibilities for computer security as laid out in the Computer Security Act of 1987.[12] The Computer Security Act requires all agencies to inventory their computer systems and to establish security plans commensurate with the sensitivity of information contained on them. Agencies are supposed to submit summaries of their security plans along with their strategic information resources management plan to the

---

[12] Appendix III does not apply to information technology that supports certain critical national security missions as defined in 44 USC 3502(9) and 10 USC 2315. National security directives to the Department of Defense have assigned policy for these national security systems, i.e., telecommunications and information systems containing classified information or used by the intelligence or military community.

Office of Management and Budget (OMB). The agencies are to follow technical, managerial, and administrative guidelines laid out by OMB, the Department of Commerce, the General Services Administration, and the Office of Personnel Management and should include (as detailed in the OMB Circular) incidence response plans, contingencies plans, and awareness and training programs for personnel. The Director of OMB may comment on those plans.

Under PDD-63, agencies submitted plans (not dissimilar in content to those called for in the Computer Security Act of 1987 and detailed in OMB Circular A-130 Appendix III) to the CIAO. The Critical Infrastructure Coordination Group assembled as expert review team to review these plans (an "ad hoc" team was set up at CIAO). What role does the Director of OMB now play in reviewing and commenting on the agency plans? What role does the National Coordinator, housed within the National Security Council and to whom the CIAO reports, play in the review and comment of an agency's security plan?[13] Who determines whether an agency's obligation to creating an adequate plan has been met?

Among the responsibilities assigned to the Department of Commerce by OMB Circular A-130 Appendix III is the coordination of agency incident response activities to promote sharing of incident response information and related vulnerabilities. This function has now migrated over to the General Services Administration which is in the process of establishing a Federal Computer Incident and Emergency Response Capability (FedCIRC). But, PDD-63 states and the National Plan reiterates that the National Infrastructure Protection Center will provide the principal means of facilitating and coordinating the federal government's response to an incident, mitigating attacks, investigating threats, and monitoring reconstitution efforts. Are the lines of authority clearly established between the different organizations many of which are tasked with doing things that sound similar? What authority or influence will the FBI, as manager of the NIPC, have over these organizations? Also, the NIPC is responsible for

---

[13] It should be noted that the General Accounting Office has reported that the oversight of agency security measures to date has been inadequate. See, U.S. General Accounting Office, Information Security. Serious Weaknesses Place Critical Federal Operations and Assets at Risk. GAO/AIMD-98-92. September 1998.

warning, responding to, and investigating intrusions. Are these functions compatible?[14]

The National Plan provides an interesting case in point. The Plan includes a discussion of the Federal Aviation Agency's (FAA) effort in establishing its own Computer Security Incident Response Capability (CSIRC), as a number of other agencies (Department of Energy, National Aeronautics and Space Administration) have done already and which is being promoted by the Directive. The CSIRC is to serve a centralized reporting and monitoring function within the FAA. It will carry our FAA-wide intrusion detection, intercepting all network activity that enters each FAA installation. It will support FAA offices by analyzing the intrusion detection data collected. There will be a Computer Incident Response Team (CIRT) trained in handling intrusions and incidents. The CIRT will also provide disaster recovery assistance to restore operations. When the CSIRC detects an intrusion, does it first inform GSA's FIDNET function or the NIPC? Does GSA's FedCIRC deal with its situation first and then forward information later? Who decides how to balance FAA's need to respond to the intrusion (say kicking the perpetrators off the network) and the FBI's need to gather sufficient evidence to catch and prosecute the perpetrators?

The Computer Security Act of 1987 also established the Computer System Security and Privacy Advisory Board (CSSPAB). The Board reports to the Secretary of Commerce and is tasked with identifying emerging issues relative to computer security and privacy, advising the National Institute of Standards and Technology and the Commerce Secretary on such issues, and reporting to the Secretary of Commerce, the Director of OMB, the Director of the National Security Agency, and appropriate congressional committees. PDD-63 establishes the National Infrastructure Assurance Council. Its duties are to propose and develop ways to encourage private industry to perform periodic risk assessments of critical processes including information and telecommunications systems and monitoring the development of private sector ISACs. The Council will report to the President through the National Coordinator and the Department of Commerce shall act as the President under the Federal Advisory Committee Act. In addition, the National Security Telecommunications Advisory Committee (NSTAC), established by Executive Order 12382 in September 1982, undertook a study back in

---

[14] This point is alluded to by Michael O'Neil, "Securing Our Critical Infrastructure: What Lurks Beyond Y2K," *Legal Times*, Week of Jan. 25, 1999.

May 1995 on the reliance of the transportation sector, the electric power sector, and the financial services sector on information networks and the risks to those sectors should those networks be compromised. Are these advisory committees/councils duplicating effort or do they offer complementary viewpoints?

There is another bureaucratic issue raised by PDD-63. Prior to the Computer Security Act of 1987, the Reagan Administration established the National Telecommunications and Information Systems Security Committee.[15] The Committee consists of 22 civilian and defense agencies. The National Security Agency was named National Manager. The Committee was tasked with setting operating policies governing the nation's telecommunications system, its classified information systems, and "other sensitive information." The Computer Security Act of 1987 was enacted in part out of congressional concern that the Committee might over-classify government-held information.[16] Does PDD-63, by couching critical infrastructures in national security terms and combining DOD and NSA professionals with civilian professionals in operative functions, blur the distinction between classified and unclassified (or national security and civilian) systems which was a primary focus of the Computer Security Act of 1987?[17]

Related to this issue is one raised by some Members of Congress who have questioned the decision to place CIAO within the Department of Commerce. To them, a threat to the nation's critical infrastructures is a national security risk and should be the responsibility of the Department of Defense. The Department of Defense did serve as the executive agent for the PCCIP's Transition Office which was to be the model for National Plan Coordinating Staff function. On the other hand, the Department of Commerce has on-going relationships with many of the private infrastructure operators with whom the Directive hopes to interact.

Restructuring by the Bush Administration. As part of its overall redesign of White House organization and assignment of responsibilities, the new Bush Administration is reviewing its options for coordinating and overseeing critical infrastructure protection. There are two parallel efforts

---

[15] National Security Decision Directive, NSDD-145. September 17, 1984.

[16] House Report 100-153(I).

[17] This point is made by the Electronic Privacy Information Center in its report, *Critical Infrastructure Protection and the Endangerment of Civil Liberties* (1998) and can be found on the Center's web page at [http://www.epic.org/security/infowar/epic-cip.html].

that impact this decision. First, the National Security Council (NSC) is undergoing a manor streamlining. All groups within the Council have been abolished and must petition for reinstatement. Whether, or to what extent, the NSC will remain the focal point for coordinating critical infrastructure protection (i.e. serve as National Coordinator and chair the Critical Infrastructure Coordination Group) is unclear. Second, there is continuing debate about the merits of establishing a government-wide Chief Information Officer, whose responsibilities would include protection of all federal non-national security-related computer systems and coordination with the private sector protection of privately owned computer systems.

There have been a number of proposals to modify the current organizational structures and responsibilities laid out in PDD-63. Various proposals would place the responsibility of overseeing and coordinating critical infrastructure directly in the White House, either dedicated to critical infrastructure or as part of a broader domestic terrorism function. Another option was put forth by the U.S. Commission on National Security/21st Century (the Hart-Rudman Commission), which proposed a new National Homeland Security Agency. The recommendation builds upon the current Federal Emergency Management Agency (FEMA) by adding to it the Coast Guard, the Border Patrol, Customs Service, and other agencies. It would include a directorate responsible for critical infrastructure protection.

In the second session of the 106th Congress, legislation was introduced that would have created a government-wide CIO and place the function outside the Office of Management and Budget (see Congressional Action below). Another option being discussed is to keep the function within OMB.

In the balance lay the future of the Critical Infrastructure Assurance Office (CIAO), which according to PDD-63 was supposed to sunset after FY2001. However, the office received a placeholder in the out-going Clinton Administration's baseline budget. Also, it remains to be seen what role the NIPC will play within the Bush Administration's efforts. The NIPC as operated by the FBI has come under some criticism for being too focused on investigations and prosecution, not equipped to integrate and analyze intelligence from a variety of sources, and unwilling to share information from its own sources.[18] That there might be problems with the functioning of

---

[18] For example, see *Bush Eyes Overhaul of E-Security*. Computer World. Vol. 34, No. 51. December 18, 2000. pp. 1,85.

the NIPC as envisioned by PDD-63 is suggested by the establishment in the summer of 2000 of the **Cyber Infrastructure Coordination Group** within the National Security Council. The Group consisted of two panels, the **Cyber Incident Working Group**, and the **Cyber Incident Steering Group**. The NIPC chaired the Working Group which included the Commander of the Joint Task Force-Computer Network Defense (the NIPC's counterpart in the Department of Defense), the chief of information operations from the National Security Agency, the director of FedCIRC, and the deputy assistant attorney general of the criminal division at the Department of Justice. This group was to review any significant computer incidents to determine the threat to U.S. economic and/or military security and to manage any federal operational response. This sounds very much like the forum the NIPC was to provide. The Group, like all others in the National Security Council, has been abolished and it remains to be seen whether it will reconstitute in some other form.

To what extent the Bush Administration commits to other critical infrastructure protection initiatives of the Clinton Administration, such as the scholarship for service program and other federal cyber service programs (see Appendix), FIDNET and FedCIRC, and research and development, also remains to be seen.

Costs. In January 2000 the Clinton Administration announced it had budgeted $2 billion in critical infrastructure protection for FY2001 (see Appendix). This is an estimate based on inputs to OMB from agencies asked to total and categorize dollars budgeted for activities related to critical infrastructure protection (e.g. systems protection, training). It is not clear, though, if agencies are consistent in what they consider relevant. Also, it is difficult to identify some of these expenditures within the agencies' budget submissions and subsequent Congressional appropriations. Much of the $2 billion is buried in other information technology or administrative line items.

Many of the agencies' activities called for immediately by the Directive will be part of on-going administrative duties. These activities, if not previously done (which appears to be the case in many agencies), will require the reallocation of personnel time and effort, presumably at the expense of other activities. The resources required to meet PDD-63 requirements are supposed to be part of the agencies' internal plans. Some of the costs will not be known until after vulnerability assessments are done and remedial actions determined. Also, each agency must develop and implement education and awareness training programs. Agency costs may not be insignificant. According to OMB, the IRS alone estimated a vulnerability analysis of its systems would cost $58 million.[19] The Plan outlines efforts at the Department of Energy to improve its network security. Total costs are expected to be $80 million ($45 million for operational security measures). On top of this, the Administration is asking for new initiatives such as the intrusion detection network (FIDNET) and education and training programs (Federal Cyber Service).

Potential private sector costs are also unknown at this time. Some sectors are already at the forefront in computer security and are sufficiently protected or need only marginal investments. Others are not and will have to devote more resources. The ability of certain sectors to raise the necessary capital may be limited, such as metropolitan water authorities which may be limited by regulation, or emergency fire which may function in a small community with limited resources. Even sectors made up of large well-capitalized firms are likely to make additional expenditures only if they can identify a net positive return on investment.

Affecting these business decisions will be issues of risk and liability. As part of its outreach efforts, the CIAO has helped the auditing, accounting, and corporate directors communities identify and present to their memberships the responsibilities governing board of directors and corporate officers have, as part of their fiduciary responsibilities, in managing the risk of their corporation's information assets. The Institute of Internal Auditors, the American Institute of Certified Public Accountants, the Information Systems Audit and Control Association and the National Association of Corporate Directors have formed a consortium and held "summits" around the country in an outreach effort. The main point of their discussion can be summed up by the following excerpt from a paper presented at these summits:

> "The consensus opinion from our analysts is that all industries and companies should be equally concerned about information technology security issues because it is an issue that has an enormous potential to negatively impact the valuation of a company's stock...it must be the responsibility of corporate leaders to ensure these threats are actually being addressed on an ongoing basis. At the

---

[19] Conversation with OMB officials, 11 February 1999.

same time, the investment community must keep the issue front and center of management."[20]

Costs to the private sector may also depend on the extent to which the private sector is compelled to go along with PDD-63 versus their ability to set their own security standards. The current thinking is the private sector should voluntarily join the effort and PDD-63 recommends that no new regulations or oversight bodies be formed. But, what happens if a sector does not take actions the federal government feels are necessary?

In an unrelated matter, but one that intersects with the efforts of critical infrastructure protection, the financial services industry and the health care industry are being required to follow new guidelines issued by their regulatory agencies aimed at protecting the privacy of their customer databases. Pursuant to the Gramm-Leach-Bliley Act of 1999, federal regulators released in February 2001, guidelines that the industry must follow. Likewise, the Bush Administration is supposed to release by this summer security rules that the health care industry must follow to comply with the 1996 Health Insurance Portability and Accountability Act (HIPPA). The guideline issued for the financial services industry are general (assess risks, have written policies and procedures to control the risk, implement and test those policies, and update them as necessary). The costs that are associated with these efforts might be a guide for what it would cost if further rules were issued related to protecting information systems upon which the nation's critical infrastructures depend.

Information Sharing. The information sharing called for in PDD-63 – internal to the federal government, between the federal government and the private sector, and between private firms – raises a number of issues.

PDD-63 calls for information to flow between agencies via FIDNET, FedCIRC and the NIPC. What kind of information will be flowing? Will reporting consist of raw network traffic data or just reports of incidents? Will content be monitored or just the packet headers?[21] Will reporting be in real-time or after-the-fact? How does this impact the privacy and confidentiality of the information provided? The Computer Matching and Privacy Protection Act of 1988 (5 U.S.C. 552a) governs the exchange of

---

[20] From a paper entitled *Information Security Impacting Securities Valuations*, by A. Marshall Acuff, Jr., Salomon Smith Barney, Inc.

[21] Information travels through the system in packets containing the information itself (content) and a header which contain addresses and instruction on how to handle the information.

records between government agencies. It is not yet clear how the goals of FIDNET and the NIPC will be impacted by the Act or how the goals of the Act may be impacted if modified to address the FIDNET and/or NIPC mission.

Since much of what is considered to be critical infrastructure is owned and operated by the private sector, implementing PDD-63 relies to a large extent on the ability of the private sector and the federal government to share information. However, it is unclear how open the private sector and the government will be in sharing information. The private sector primarily wants from the government information on potential threats which the government may want to protect in order not to compromise sources or investigations. In fact, much of the threat assessment done by the federal government is considered classified.[22] For its part, the government wants specific information on intrusions which companies may hold as proprietary or which they may want to protect to prevent adverse publicity. Success will depend on the ability of each side to demonstrate it can hold in confidence the information exchanged.

This issue is made more complex by the question of how the information exchanged will be handled within the context of the Freedom of Information Act (FOIA). Proponents of PDD-63 would hope to exempt the information from public disclosure under the existing FOIA statute. Those more critical of the Directive are concerned that PDD-63 will expand the government's ability to hold more information as classified or sensitive.[23]

Another question has been raised about the FBI's INFRAGARD program. For example, are firms who volunteer to participate in the program given additional or better information than what is available through the FBI outside the program?

Finally, the information exchanged between private firms within the context of the Sector Coordinators and the ISACS raises antitrust concerns, as well as concerns about sharing information that might unduly benefit competitors.

---

[22] There are precedents for sharing classified information with private infrastructure operators, and it has been mentioned that these situations might be a model for sharing such information with ISACs and their members, if proper controls are in place. This, however, may involve additional expense and procedural issues for those industries or firms not familiar with handling such information.

[23] Op. cit. EPIC.

Privacy/Civil Liberties? The PDD states that individual liberties and rights to privacy are to be preserved as the Directive is implemented. However, on-line monitoring, either for system management reasons or for intrusion detection, has the potential to collect vast amounts of information on who is doing what on the network. Once an intrusion is detected, the federal government could get involved in real-time monitoring. What, if any, of that information should be treated as private and subject to privacy laws?

The National Plan states that it is the intent of the Clinton Administration to pass all critical infrastructure efforts through the lens of privacy issues. In addition to promised vigorous and thorough legal reviews of Plan programs, the Plan proposes an annual colloquium on Cyber Security, Civil Liberties, and Citizens' Rights between the representatives of the federal government and outside groups.

But members of the privacy and civil liberty communities remain concerned about proposals that have been made. For example, the PCCIP recommended that law enforcement officials should need to get only a single warrant to track hackers through cyberspace, rather than having to get a new warrant every time they trace a hacker to a computer in another jurisdiction. The PCCIP also recommended that employers be allowed to administer polygraph tests to their computer security personnel. There are also suggestions of requiring background checks for computer security personnel. The Clinton Administration did not take a position on any of these recommendations. However, in a hearing before the House Judiciary's Subcommittee on Crime (February 29, 2000), the Clinton Administration did say that having a nationwide track and trace capability would be very helpful in identifying hackers.

Another issue is to what extent will monitoring and responding to cyber attacks permit the government to get involved in the day-to-day operations of private infrastructures? The PCCIP suggested possibly modifying the Defense Production Act (50 USC Appendix, 2061 *et seq*) to provide the federal government with the authority to direct private resources to help reconstitute critical infrastructures suffering from cyber attack. This authority exists now regarding the supply and distribution of energy and critical materials in an emergency. Suppose that the computer networks managing the nation's railroads were to "go down" for unknown but suspicious reasons. What role would the federal government play in allocating resources and reconstituting service?

CONGRESSIONAL ACTION

Congress's interest in protecting the nation's critical infrastructure pans its oversight, legislative, and appropriating responsibilities. Most Congressional activity regarding critical infrastructure protection has focused to date on oversight. A number of committees have held hearing on various aspects of the issue. These include the Senate Judiciary's Subcommittee on Technology, Terrorism and Government Information and the Subcommittee on Criminal Justice Oversight, the House Judiciary's Subcommittee on Crime, the Senate Committee on Small Business, the House Science Committee's Technology Subcommittee, the House Government Reform Committee's Subcommittee on Government Management, Information, and Technology, which in September 2000, released a report card rating how well agencies were protecting their information assets.

While there was much activity administratively, on the part of the Clinton Administration, and in oversight by the Congress, legislation has moved more slowly.

In the 106th Congress a number of bills were introduced that addressed one or another issued associated with PDD-63. A couple bills were directly related to PDD-63. S.2702 required the President to report to Congress on the specific actions being taken by agencies to implement PDD-63. This requirement was later added as an amendment to the FY2001 Department of Defense Authorization Act (P.L. 106-398). H.R. 4246 directly addressed FOIA and anti-trust concerns associated with ISACs by defining a "cyber security web site" and exempting those websites from FOIA access and anti-trust litigation as long as information contained on those sites are not used to impede free market functions. Also, the bill explicitly allowed the federal government to set up working groups of federal officials to work with industry groups without such groups being considered as federal advisory committees.

Other bills dealt more with computer security in general. S.1993 amended Chapter 35 USC 44 (related to the Paperwork Reduction Act), to strengthen information security practices throughout the federal government by adding a separate subchapter specifically dedicated to information security. Among other things, the bill requires agencies to have an annual outside assessment of their computer security plans and practices and calls on the Comptroller General to report on those reviews. The bill was attached to the FY2001 Defense Authorization Act (Title X, Subtitle G (referred to as the Government Information Security Reform Act in P.L. 106-398)). H.R. 5024 would have transferred many of the computer security given the Director of OMB by the Paperwork Reduction Act of 1995 to a Government-wide Chief Information Officer located outside OMB.

A number of other bills were introduced that addressed issues such as applying trap and trace procedures to tracking hackers across jurisdictions, modifying thresholds and penalties in computer crime statutes, and organizational changes meant to deal better with computer crime and cyber-terrorism. Also, there have been and continue to be a number of other bills introduced that relate to privacy, encryption, public key policies, computer fraud, etc. These issues are tangentially related to PDD-63.[24]

The 107th Congress will undoubtedly continue its oversight of the efforts to protect the nation's critical infrastructure. Also, there may be legislation introduced associated with restructuring the responsibilities for overseeing and coordinating Administration efforts and/or legislation reexamining the criminal statutes and those relating to criminal investigations.

APPENDIX

FY2001 Budget

On January 7, 2000, the Clinton Administration announced it was going to ask for $2.03 billion in FY2001 for protecting the nation's critical infrastructure against cyber attacks. This was an estimate by OMB, based on canvassing individual agencies to identify activities that constitute protection of their critical infrastructure or support the protection of infrastructure in the private sector. Included in the tally was $621 million for research and development, up from the $461 million that Congress appropriated for FY2000. Among the highlights mentioned in the announcement were a number of initiatives listed below.

---

[24] For an overview of these issues, see Congressional Research Service. *Internet: An Overview of Six Key Policy Issues Affecting Its Use and Growth*, by Marcia Smith et al. CRS Report 98-67 STM. Updated, April 9, 1999.

Federal Cyber Services Training and Education ($25 million)

This initiative is an effort to improve the recruitment and retention of a highly skilled government information technology workforce, including increasing the pool of skilled information security specialists. The initiative consists of a number of different activities.

One activity would be a ROTC-like program where the federal government, through the National Science Foundation (NSF), will pay for a 2-year undergraduate or graduate degree in information security in exchange for government service in information security, called the Scholarship for Service (SFS). The scholarship would be for two years at schools with accredited information technology programs. Students participating in the program would also do summer internships at government agencies and attend periodic conferences.

A second activity is called the Center for Information Technology Excellence (CITE). CITE would provide continuing training for existing federal systems administrators and information systems security officers. CITE will be managed and run by the Office of Personnel Management. Training will be offered by selected sites both inside and outside the federal government. Curricula will be based on key competencies and a certification process will demonstrate that those competencies have been demonstrated. It should be noted that the National Security Agency runs 8 universities as centers of information technology excellence. The CITE program identified here would use the experience of the NSA program to establish a similar capability for the entire federal government.

A third activity would be a high school and secondary school outreach program to educate high school students and teachers and the general public about information security. The fourth activity would be to promote information security awareness within the federal workforce.

Permanent Expert Review Team ($5 million over two years)

This would make permanent the review of agencies' internal security plans, vulnerability analyses, etc. The team would be supported through the National Institute of Standards and Technology.

Federal Intrusion Detection Network ($10 million)

FIDNET would be an intrusion detection network for civilian government agencies managed by the General Services Administration. It should be noted that the Department of Defense and the National Security Agency have each set up their own intrusion detection networks. These will all be linked together and with the National Infrastructure Protection Center at the FBI.

Public Key Infrastructure Pilots ($7 million)

Public key infrastructure (PKI) allows two-way authentication of communications over computers and is critical for electronic commerce and for agency to exchange information with contractors, constituents, etc. This initiative would support 7 pilot programs at different federal agencies.

Institute for Information Infrastructure Protection ($50 million)

This would be a research and development fund operated through the National Institute of Standards and Technology (NIST) to support research that might not otherwise be conducted by the private sector or defense agencies. Currently nearly all of the current information security research and development funds go to defense agencies. While operated through NIST, the Institute would report to a Federal Coordinating Council consisting of the President's Science Advisor, the Deputy Director/Office of Management and Budget, the Director/National Security Agency, the Director/NIST, and the National Coordinator for Security, Infrastructure Protection, and Counter-Terrorism. The Institute would consult with the National Infrastructure Advisory Council and the Sector Coordinators.

Since much of the estimated $2.0 billion budgeted for critical infrastructure protection falls within ongoing administrative accounts, it is difficult to track the extent of which these activities are supported by appropriations until (or unless) OMB releases a FY2002 budget identifying how expenditures were allocated in FY2001. However, a couple of initiatives were more highly visible and Congress provided mixed support for them. For example, the NSF scholarship for service program received its $11.2 million appropriation. NIST did not receive the $50 million appropriation for the Institute for Information Infrastructure Protection, but did receive $3 million of the $5 million requested for the Expert Review Team. GSA received $8 million of the $15 million it requested for FIDNET and FedCIRC. How much of that goes toward FIDNET is not clear.

Table A.1. Critical Infrastructure Protection Funding by Department (millions $)

Department	FY98 Actual	FY99 Actual	FY00 Enacted	FY01 request
Agriculture	2.70	3.22	3.88	14.03
Commerce	9.35	21.81	17.75	92.10
Education	3.59	4.45	5.23	2.51
Energy	1.50	3.60	21.98	45.30
EOP	0.05	0.58	0.48	0.56
EPA	0.12	0.24	0.08	2.3
FEMA	0.00	0.00	0.80	1.47
GSA	0.00	3.00	0.00	15.40
HHS	21.83	12.17	13.17	19.55
Interior	1.29	1.60	2.65	1.83
Justice	25.61	54.09	44.02	45.51
NASA	41.00	43.00	66.00	61.00
NSF	19.15	21.42	26.65	43.85
National Security (incl. DOD)	974.56	1,185.22	1,402.94	1,458.91
Nuclear Regulatory Commission	0.00	0.20	0.00	0.25
OPM	0.00	0.00	2.00	9.00
Transportation	20.33	24.88	50.68	92.34
Treasury	22.91	48.89	76.22	87.03
Veteran's Affairs	0.00	0.00	17.33	17.39
Grand Total	**1,143.98**	**1,428.35**	**1,751.86**	**2,010.33**

Data from Office of Management and Budget

INDEX